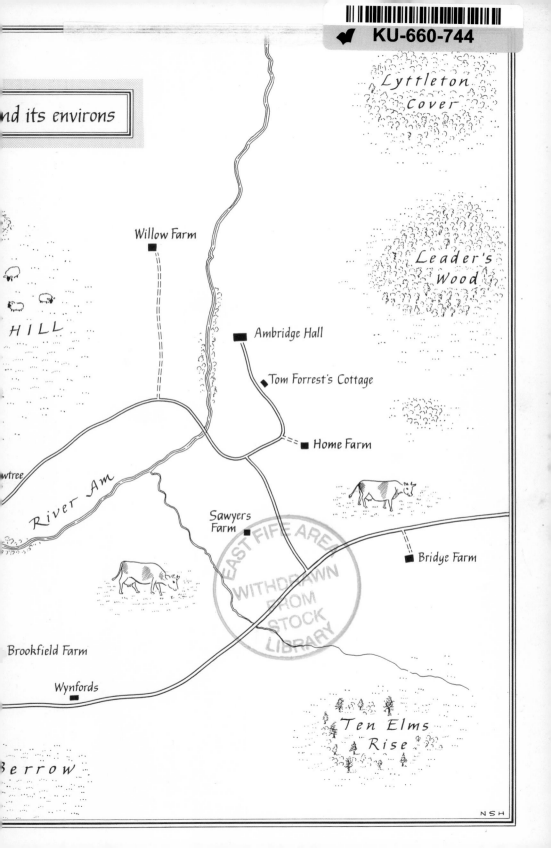

...nd its environs

KU-660-744

EAST FIFE AREA WITHDRAWN FROM STOCK LIBRARY

Lyttleton Cover

Leader's Wood

Willow Farm

HILL

Ambridge Hall

Tom Forrest's Cottage

Home Farm

...wtree

River Am

Sawyers Farm

Bridye Farm

Brookfield Farm

Wynfords

Ten Elms Rise

...errow

NSH

THE ARCHERS

The first thirty years

THE ARCHERS

The first thirty years

Edited by

WILLIAM SMETHURST

Eyre Methuen
By Arrangement with the British Broadcasting Corporation

First published in 1980 by
Eyre Methuen Ltd
11 New Fetter Lane, London EC4P 4EE
Copyright © William Smethurst 1980
Filmset, printed and bound in Great Britain
by Hazell Watson & Viney Ltd,
Aylesbury, Bucks

British Library Cataloguing in Publication Data

'The Archers', the first thirty years.
1. Archers, The (Radio program)
I. Smethurst, William
791.44'7   PN1991.77.A7

ISBN 0-413-47830-0

NORTH EAST FIFE DISTRICT LIBRARY	
CLASS	791.444
COPY	1
VENDOR	A
PURCHASE DATE	11/80
PRICE	£5.95

Acknowledgements

Photographs on pages 30 and 145 are printed by courtesy of the *Birmingham Post and Mail*, and on page 63 by courtesy of the *Oxford Mail*. Photographs on pages 18, 36, 40, 54, 56, 60, 83, 99, 101, 103, 155, 165, 167, 170 and 175 are by permission of the BBC; on pages 46 and 50 by permission of the Radio Times Hulton Picture Library; and on page 15 by permission of the *Daily Mirror*. Photographs on pages 136, 140, 151 and 152 are by Harry Smith, and other photographs are by members of the cast and production team.

The passage on page 80 is quoted by permission of the editor of *The Times*; and the passage on page 93 by permission of the editor of the *Sunday Telegraph*.

Contents

The Archers of Ambridge

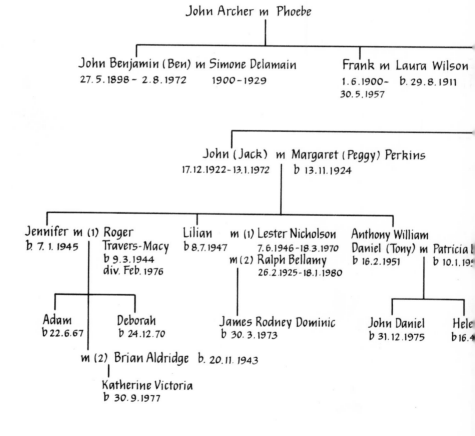

John Archer m Phoebe

John Benjamin (Ben) m Simone Delamain
27.5.1898 – 2.8.1972   1900–1929

Frank m Laura Wilson
1.6.1900– b. 29.8.1911
30.5.1957

John (Jack) m Margaret (Peggy) Perkins
17.12.1922–13.1.1972 b 13.11.1924

Jennifer m (1) Roger
b. 7. 1. 1945   Travers-Macy
b 9.3.1944
div. Feb. 1976

Lilian   m (1) Lester Nicholson
b 8.7.1947   7.6.1946–18.3.1970
m (2) Ralph Bellamy
26.2.1925–18.1.1980

Anthony William
Daniel (Tony) m Patricia
b 16.2.1951   b 10.1.19

Adam
b 22.6.67

Deborah
b 24.12.70

James Rodney Dominic
b 30. 3. 1973

John Daniel
b 31.12.1975

Hele
b 16.4

m (2) Brian Aldridge b. 20.11. 1943

Katherine Victoria
b 30.9.1977

William Forrest m Lisa

Daniel m Doris
b 15.10.1896 | b 11.7.1900

Edward George (Ted)
10.1.1902 – 17.1.1920

Thomas William (Tom) b 20.10.1910
m
Prudence Harris (Pru) b 27.7.1921

Philip Walter m (1) Grace Fairbrother
b 23.4.1928   2.4.1929 – 22.9.1955
m (2) Jill Patterson
b 3.10.1930

Christine m (1) Paul Johnson
b 21.12.1931 | 10.1.1931 – 10.5.1978

Shula Mary
b 8.8.1958

Kenton Edward
b 8.8.1958

David Thomas
b 18.9.1959

Elizabeth
b 21.4.1967

Peter (adopted)
b 5.9.1965

m (2) George Barford
24.10.1928

The Fifties

CHAPTER 1

The Archers' Story I

by Jock Gallagher,
Head of Radio, BBC Pebble Mill

Twenty million words have been spoken in Ambridge since Dan and Doris Archer were first introduced to a British radio audience. Since then the Archers and their friends and neighbours have become as familiar to listeners as any of their own relatives.

But The Archers did not spring to life fully-formed. It developed in true BBC fashion, documented at every turn, and in a mountain of yellowing flimsies (often in quadruplicate and never less than in duplicate), BBC admin men and women have left an astonishing – and continuing – history of the BBC's most successful radio serial.

'Mr Dan Archer of Wimberton Farm, Little Twittington?' It might have happened. Little Twittington was put forward as a possible name for Ambridge, and it was Wimberton Farm, not Brookfield, in the programme's first trial run in 1950.

The programme was conceived, not long after the Second World War had ended, by Godfrey Baseley, who was then producing agricultural programmes at the BBC's Midland Region studios in Birmingham, and the correspondence between him and Head Office (as Broadcasting House, London, was then styled) clearly captures the austerity of the forties. After nearly two years' battling to get his idea accepted, Godfrey finally got down to the logistics of launching The Archers. At once, he found himself up against the problem that still haunts BBC producers – shortage of cash. He had estimated that the cost of each fifteen-minute episode would be about £55: that was to cover writers, actors, studio operators and secretarial help! His London masters, however, were not impressed. In the end, he was allowed £47. A somewhat cool memo made it clear that he would have to manage as best he could, while insisting at the same time that 'no artiste should be paid less than ten guineas a week for the repertory contract'. (Such a contract was only offered to the main actors and actresses and guaranteed them work for three months.)

Although the BBC has a reputation for keeping meticulous records of all its doings, the amazing detail of the history of The Archers lies, one suspects, in the programme's original *raison d'être* – propaganda – and its consequent involvement with Whitehall, bastion of bureaucracy. The idea stemmed from Godfrey Baseley's concern that not enough farmers – and particularly the smaller farmers – were listening to his specialized information programmes at a time when Britain desperately needed to increase food-production. Godfrey had been a staff speaker with the wartime Ministry of Information, and having exhorted gardeners to dig for victory, he knew the value of propaganda (which was then, of course, a perfectly respectable word). Even more important, he knew when it was not hitting its target. In an effort to put things right, Godfrey persuaded his newly-appointed boss, John Dunkerley, Controller of the BBC's Midland Region, to call a meeting of farmers to see if any new ideas might be forthcoming.

On Thursday, 3 June 1948, the meeting was held, under the chairmanship of John Dunkerley, in the Birmingham City Council Chamber, a suitably splendid backcloth for the many distinguished figures who attended. After the chairman's opening remarks, the first speakers were Professor H. G. Robinson of Nottingham University and a Mr Christopher Norbury, a fruit farmer from Worcestershire. Many others followed, but still nothing new seemed to be forthcoming until another farmer, Mr Henry Burtt from Lincolnshire, disrupted the proceedings with his assertion that what was needed to get the message across was 'a farming *Dick Barton*'. The rather staid assembly guffawed because *Dick Barton* was then the derring-do hero of an action-packed radio serial which had a regular and almost fanatical audience of nearly four million. But Godfrey Baseley saw the potential, and spent most of the following two years trying to convince others that a daily fifteen-minute drama serial was the perfect propaganda vehicle.

Finally he was given the go-ahead – but only for a week's trial run on the Midland Home Service. Godfrey, with that 'farming *Dick Barton*' probably still in his mind, turned to his old friend, Edward

J. Mason, who was in fact co-writer, with Geoffrey Webb, of *Dick Barton*, and asked if he might be interested in writing the script. Ted Mason agreed on the understanding that Geoff Webb, himself a countryman, should also be involved. And so began a collaboration that would become one of the most successful in the history of radio.

In Whit week, 1950, listeners to the Midland Home Service heard for the first time about a farming family in the little Borsetshire village of Ambridge. The family was called Archer and was made up of Daniel and Doris, their three children, Jack, Philip and Christine, and their daughter-in-law, Jack's wife, Peggy. The only other Ambridge inhabitants heard during that week were Daniel's farm-hand, Simon Cooper, and a near-neighbour, Walter Gabriel.

If one went by audience figures alone, the trial might well have been deemed unsuccessful. Not too many people heard the five episodes, with a later estimate suggesting that the figure was as low as fifty thousand. But then, with its record of public service broadcasting, the BBC was less influenced by figures and more by the response

The first photograph of The Archers' cast, taken in December 1950. Left to right, back row: Godfrey Baseley, Tony Shryane, Leslie Bowmar, June Spencer, Denis Folwell, Monica Grey, Eddie Robinson; front row: Christine Willson, Robert Mawdesley, Pamela Mant, Gwen Berryman, Harry Oakes, Norman Painting, Deidre Alexander.

of those who had listened. Since this had been good, Godfrey Baseley soon found allies in the next stage of his campaign – to get the
serial on to the nationally-heard Light Programme.

With the backing of John Dunkerley and the Midland Programme
Head, Denis Morris (later to become Head of Light Programme),
Godfrey had those first five episodes, recorded on enormous acetate
discs, sent to London. The initial response was cool. The controller
of the Light Programme was T. W. Chalmers and he wrote to Denis
Morris: 'It will be no easy matter to convince DHB (Director, Home
Broadcasting, the equivalent of today's Managing Director, Radio)
that we should give national coverage to yet another family pro-
gramme.' (At the time, 'family' shows, included *Mrs Dale's Diary*,
The Robinson Family and *Life with the Lyons*.)

Mr Chalmers was not actually dismissing the programme which,
in any case, he had not then heard. He was simply indulging in the
safety procedures and keeping his options open. There was also a
strong hint that there was still a long way to go, when he asked for
'an appreciation of the serial, i.e. the general plan, analysis of characters, policy musts and mustn'ts.' His memo was written at the end
of July 1950 and, despite the intervening bank holiday, he had on his
desk within ten days the document which was to become central to
the enduring success of The Archers. It was Godfrey Baseley's exposition and declaration of intent:

PURPOSE
To present an accurate picture of country life and in so doing draw
portraits of typical country people and follow them at work and at
play and to eavesdrop on the many problems of living that con-
front country folk in general.

PRESENTATION
In play form, with all the characters played by actors.

POLICY
The most important thing here is accuracy. To keep a good balance
between the purely factual and the more entertaining aspects of
country life and to keep in mind always that the programme be
directed to the general listener, ie the townsman, and through the
entertainment develop an appreciation of the inexhaustible diver-
sions to be found in the countryside. These to be kept as topical
and seasonal as possible. For instance, should any important country matter be discussed in the House of Commons, we should
include the natural reactions of our characters to this subject.

CHARACTERS
As the small farmer is the hard core of the rural population, I

believe it is important to make our principal character representative of this class. He would be progressive in a quiet way, always anxious to follow latest developments, so far as finance and practical experience will allow. His wife, a country girl, left school at fourteen in good service with county family until she married, now striving to do the best she can for her family of three. As the farm prospers, so she develops, slowly, her social position. The eldest son, ex-army, married a town girl in the services, now on a small-holding partially paid for by gratuity money, fighting hard to make a living for his growing family on four or five acres, with glasshouses. The second son received a little better education at the grammar school, but failed School Certificate; now apprenticed to an agricultural engineer and 'courting' the daughter of a much bigger farmer in the district. The younger daughter, still at grammar school, has prospects of winning a county major scholarship which will give her entry to university or agricultural college.

In addition to the above, the squire and his wife would be included; they own the majority of the village and surrounding countryside and are the leaders of village life generally – Women's Institutes, Girl Guides, Scouts, Parish Council, Village Hall, etc. Another important character would be the neighbour farmer, who is 'agin' most things. Fairly naturally in their place, as the situation demanded, would come the policeman, district nurse, bank manager, town visitors, local or visiting naturalists, the parson, the publican and the postmistress.

Having read that and having heard the trial programmes, Mr Chalmers became, if not exactly enthusiastic, certainly less cool: 'I must confess that I was far more favourably impressed than I had expected.' He took the proposition to his boss and by 15 September 1950 he was writing again to Denis Morris in Birmingham: 'I am glad to tell you that DHB's reaction to my presentation of the case of The Archers was favourable. There is no hurry about starting it, and before we commit ourselves finally, I should like to have a careful estimate of the cost.'

The cost of the operation was to be the last hurdle for Godfrey Baseley, and his Birmingham colleagues. They accepted the London figure of £47 for each of the fifteen-minute episodes and set up a streamlined programme unit that would have won the approval of even the most penny-pinching, cost-conscious accountant. The only full-time member of the unit was to be the clerk/typist and she was to be paid £6 a week out of the programme allowance. Godfrey was to act as editor 'being responsible for policy, acceptance of scripts

and any trouble that might arise' and that, it was reckoned, would
take him a full day a week! For the rest of the week he continued
with his other duties. It was also agreed that 'on a trial basis, a
member of the programme engineering or studio-managing staff be
used as junior producer.' The lucky candidate was Tony Shryane.
With Mason, Webb and Baseley, Shryane was to become the other
name so familiar to listeners: 'The Archers, written by Edward J.
Mason and Geoffrey Webb, was edited by Godfrey Baseley and produced by Tony Shryane.' That was the credit heard by listeners at
the end of every programme right up to 1962, when Geoffrey Webb
died. In 1950, the team was bound together by endless enthusiasm
and energy, qualities that were essential in sustaining them in the
battle to get *their* programme into the front-line of British broadcasting. As it happened, each of the four had additional personal
needs for The Archers to be successful. Godfrey wanted to show that
he had found a way to help the farmers; Ted and Geoff were determined to show the versatility of their writing talents; and for Tony

The original production team – left to right, Tony Shryane (producer),
Godfrey Baseley (editor), Edward J. Mason and Geoffrey Webb (script-
writers) in 1954.

Shryane, it represented a heaven-sent opportunity to break into programme-making.

The first hint that their chances of success were high came in fact from one of broadcasting's most colourful personalities, the late Franklin Engelmann. Jingle, as he was known to his friends, was in charge of the Light Programme's presentation and one of his responsibilities was to vet scripts. He was sent The Archers' script about a month before it was due for transmission and his assessment was unequivocal. 'I have read the first five episodes of this and I think that it is a first-class job. Maybe I have got more interest in the country than most people, but I feel pretty confident that in spite of its specialist angles, it will have a very, very wide appeal.'

That was it. The programme was cleared for take-off. At 11.45 am on 1 January 1951, after a short burst of the now-famous signature tune, Britain had its first introduction to The Archers of Ambridge.

Theme in and down for

ANNOUNCER: The Archers. An everyday story of country folk.
Theme up and out under
The Archers are country folk – farmers. Dan Archer, the head of the family, his wife Doris, younger son Philip and daughter Christine, live at Brookfield Farm. The other son, Jack, and his wife Peggy live on the outskirts of Ambridge village and run a small market garden. The Archers are children of the soil and like most work-a-day folk they have their joys and troubles, their ups and downs. But we join them at a moment when all tribulations are forgotten, when families unite to celebrate a memorable occasion – seeing the New Year in.
Fade in on family informally singing Auld Lang Syne.

DAN: And a Happy New Year to all!
General exchange of greetings.

DORIS: (*Quietly*) A very happy New Year, Dan.

DAN: Thanks, mother. If it's as good as the last 'un I'll be satisfied.

JACK: How about some more of that rich and ripe old cooking port, Dad?

DAN: That's no cooking port, Jack. You've got no palate on you. Your mother bought that at old Mrs Benson's sale two years ago, and goodness only knows how long it had been lay down in her cellar.

JACK:	Doesn't seem to have been lying down with very good company.
DORIS:	Really, Jack!
DAN:	Never mind Jack, mother. It's good enough for me. And now we've all got our glasses filled, here's a toast.
PHILIP:	(*Pompous*) Pray silence for the lord and master of Brookfield Farm and Sire of the Illustrious Family of Archer and – and—
CHRISTINE:	Shut up, Philip.
DAN:	(*Serious*) Doris, Christine, Jack, Philip, Peggy – and that includes your two youngsters, me dear, and the one on the way – I – oh, and I mustn't forget you, Miss Fairbrother. Well – all of you – I haven't got much to say, but – somehow—
PHILIP:	You're going to take a long time saying it.
DAN:	(*Good-natured*) Shut up, Philip, you're putting me off. All I want to say is – here's to the coming year and may we all get what we're after, may we go on being as happy and united a family as we've been up to now – and may the weather be a bit kinder to all farmers. *Hear hears and laughter*
JACK:	And here's to mother. *Hear hear* May her shadow never get leaner – God bless her. *Hear hear*
DORIS:	Thank you, children.
GRACE:	May I say something, Mrs Archer?
DORIS:	Why, of course, Grace. Anybody's free to speak here, dear.
GRACE:	I just wanted to say I – I hope you'll always be here – and that I'll be able to – to – (*Tears in her voice*) Oh, I'm sorry. I can't go on. I always get like this on New Year's Eve.
DAN:	Never mind, Miss Fairbrother. There is something sad about the old year going out – but it's gone now. It's the first of January and nigh on another working day. Time we packed it all up and went to bed.

The original cast was: Dan, Harry Oakes; Doris, Gwen Berryman; Philip, Norman Painting; Christine, Pamela Mant; Jack, Denis Folwell; Peggy, June Spencer; Grace Fairbrother, Monica Grey; Walter Gabriel, Robert Mawdesley and Simon, Eddie Robinson. Of those nine members, three are still with the programme thirty years later: Norman Painting (who also had a long spell writing scripts under the pseudonym Bruno Milna), June Spencer and Gwen Berryman.

At this stage, the new programme was still very much on trial – officially for three months – and it was the initial uncertainty about the length of the programme's run that, in fact, led to 'Barwick Green' becoming the signature tune. In a memo to his London boss during the planning stages, a Birmingham administrator added a PS. 'While you were here, Baseley was a little too diffident to raise the question of special music. What he wants is a specially-composed opening sequence and closing sequence, together with a number of musical punctuations. Going by previous experience, the kind of thing he wants (with nearly full orchestral resources) would cost between £250 and £350, taking all rights. This can't come out of the budget for the thirteen-week trial run. Are you game to float it on a speculative basis?'

The gentleman was not game and Godfrey had to resort to poring over dozens of gramophone records. Among them he found Arthur Wood's catchy little tune.

There was little doubt about the almost instant success of The Archers. Within weeks, it had built an audience of two million. The Light Programme listeners took Dan (the Daniel tag was quickly dropped in favour of the diminutive), Doris, their family and friends to their hearts – and that was what the BBC bosses were waiting for: confirmation of their own instincts. The 'trial' label was dropped and the programme was given a better placing. As from Easter Monday, 2 April 1951, it was broadcast in peak-listening time at 6.45 pm. Ironically enough, the programme killed to make way for it was *Dick Barton*. The laughter that had followed Henry Burtt's suggestion of nearly three years earlier now sounded very hollow. While Dan Archer was not exactly a farming *Dick Barton*, he certainly proved an equally popular substitute to the wireless audience.

By the end of the first week of evening broadcasts, The Archers had doubled its audience, to more than four million, adding nearly half-a-million to those who had listened to *Dick Barton*. Television, of course, was still in its infancy and was on the air for only four or five hours a day, with much of the time taken up by news and current affairs. Roy Plomley did have his controversial programme *We Beg to Differ*, in which the participants included Joyce Grenfell, Gilbert Harding, Bernard Braden and Barbara Kelly, and there was a variety show called *The Top Hat* which gave us the famous dancing girls, The Toppers, and featured Arthur English, but none of that offered serious competition. All the competition was on the wireless itself.

In addition to the family programmes mentioned earlier, there was an amazing choice for listeners. Wilfred Pickles extended his weekly invitation to *Have a Go*, with Mabel at the piano; Billy Cotton bawled his way through his *Band Show* and dominated Sundays with his 'Wakey, Wakey' and wisecracks about lead singer, Alan Breeze; Brian Reece contributed to the 'aren't-our-policemen-wonderful' image with *The Adventures of PC 49*; Sandy Macpherson offered a bit of uplift with his *Chapel in the Valley*; and Henry Wood added a touch of class with his *Promenade Concerts*. There were many more and to join such company and soar to the dizzy heights of audience-ratings was no mean feat. Even the cautious London bosses were beginning to think that there might just be a future for The Archers.

At the first script conference after the programme was broadcast on the Light Programme, it had been agreed that the move to the new evening timing should be regarded as the beginning of a new serial, 'with Dan Archer as the central figure and Brookfield Farm as the centre of activity. The microphone need not move down to the smallholding (worked by Jack) so often.' In addition to the programme team, the meeting was attended by the Assistant Head of Midland Region's Programmes, David Gretton, and the Assistant Head of Light Programme, John McMillan. The minutes are brief but informative.

Mr Baseley said that, from his point of view, Peggy and Jack represent the longings and desires of millions of people. However, it was agreed that the story should focus on Dan and the rest weave around this central theme.

Another point that Mr McMillan made was that there should be no indelicacies. Also, if there is a suitable English equivalent for the word, no Americanisms.

It seemed that a little more rural activity was needed and there are plenty of rural problems that Dan could be involved in. It was decided that fifteen per cent instruction is sufficient, as the first object of the programme is to entertain.

Everyone agreed that different music should be used between scenes and the breaks must not be too long.

Finally, it was decided to hold a script conference each time there is a new story to be considered.

This was to be the pattern for the future, with always the same concern for propriety and always the same precision: 'Fifteen per cent instruction, etc.' The audience, of course, knew nothing of such discussions, but they have undoubtedly played some part in the success of the programme. So too has the passionate concern consistently shown by the Corporation's hierarchy, although it could not have been easy for the programme people to receive memos such as the one instructing them to remove the following two lines of dialogue, which took place in a conversation at Brookfield before Dan and Doris Archer went on a coach trip.

DORIS: Would you like another cup of tea before we go?
DAN: No. No thanks, Doris. You know what I'm like on coaches.

Another memo ran as follows:

I wonder if you would be good enough to consider the vicar as represented by Ted Mason and Geoffrey Webb. I have not actually heard him but I have read the scripts in which he appears and am disappointed that the writers should have chosen to re-create a musical comedy character.

If I am right, could we please have a new vicar who is active and worldly-wise. The Church is very seldom represented regularly in radio drama and it seems a pity that on this occasion we should choose someone who is quite obviously unrepresentative.

Because of its source, Godfrey Baseley's response was restrained. He said he did not agree but would 'watch it' in future.

When, a few weeks later, he received another note, his response was less restrained. 'I was down in the West on Friday night,' said the writer, 'and the local yokels were being scornful about The Archers, I am sorry to say. However, they only had one detailed criticism. This was that recently a one-year-old heifer slipped a calf. Apparently, heifers of this delicate age are not allowed to get in that interesting condition. Would you care to comment?' Yes, Godfrey cared. He cared very much that his almost-obsessive attention to detail was being questioned. 'In reply to your memo of May 15th, a heifer is a yearling until it is two years of age. In the Midlands, it is a regular practice to mate at 15–18 months old, so as to calve round two years of age, then suckle for three months, then fatten and be sold to the Ministry of Food under grade "cow heifer". This is quite authentic and it's time the yokels in the West grew up.'

It says much for the sense of the BBC hierarchy that the matter was dropped without further comment. If a programme-maker is doing a good job, as Godfrey Baseley was so clearly doing, there is no demand for him or her unduly to stand on ceremony – which is wonderful for students of history, because it makes some of the memos and letters so much more interesting.

The yokels referred to in this exchange were in fact BBC staff in the West Region studios at Bristol and the use of the word, in a way, highlights the often-mistaken view that London administrators have of their provincial colleagues. For example, in 1950 the men in the metropolis might have thought they had shown their superiority in beating down Godfrey Baseley's £55-a-programme bid when he was trying to float his idea, but by the summer of 1951, with the audience figures building nicely, they learned their error. Godfrey had pulled the time-honoured regional trick of getting the programme on the air at London's price and waiting for an opportune moment to strike back for more sensible financing. He turned on the dripping-tap: could he have an increase in the weekly budget? Could an additional script-writer be slowly introduced? And, of course, could London find the money, please? Yes, yes. Then another twist, this time on the staffing side. The following note was sent from one administrator in Birmingham, to another in London: 'We have bumped up against a rather awkward staffing problem, as it concerns the production of The Archers and after full consideration, I am wondering whether you can help in meeting the cost of the following proposition?' The awkward staffing problem was that the production of the five-days-a-week serial was, perhaps not surprisingly, taking up rather more of Tony Shryane's time than originally estimated and, as he was only meant to be released part-time from his other duties, it was throwing a strain on the Programme Operations department. The proposal was that Tony become the full-time producer and that London pay the subsequent bills, for his extra salary and that of his replacement. It is on such nerve that whole empires are built. London agreed but added, somewhat hopelessly: 'If there is any likelihood that your staffing problems will have become eased . . . perhaps there is just the possibility that you can release the operator . . . thus relieving us of the additional cost.' It is easy to see that the writer knew he had lost.

   The next round, however, certainly went to the London Head Office men. After a long meeting, Godfrey wrote a memo to the London programme head (who had been at the meeting) which purported to be the minutes. Somewhere in the middle was a proposal for an omnibus edition of the programme and the apparently unanimous feeling that this should go ahead. This is another classic ploy: send a long detailed note to a very busy man, hope that he will not have time to read it properly but that he will simply acknowledge it, and then later use the acknowledgement as evidence of agreement. But this time it did not work. The reply came back, 'I cannot remember having discussed the possibility at any length . . . I am not prepared to recommend that we should try an omnibus edition of The

Archers at this stage.' But Godfrey hardly noticed the rebuff. His enthusiasm was undented and every time anyone mentioned the word omnibus, another note dropped on to a London desk.

Meanwhile, it was back to the meticulous planning and the long, long discussions. One script conference, on Hallowe'en night, was held in the Birmingham pub called The Hope and Anchor, a name that somehow seemed to exactly capture the spirit of the day. From the minutes of the meeting, it is clear that the programme-makers felt the need for the odd touch on the rudder:

GENERAL PATTERN AND TONE OF THE PROGRAMME
It was suggested that more reference back to the original plans of the programme should be made, as it was felt that there was a tendency to move away from these.

It was agreed that the speed of the action in the serial should be thirty per cent slower.

It was felt that the location of scenes should be thirty per cent more at Brookfield Farm, and that the characters could make use of the pub as their community centre, so long as drink (alcoholic) was not predominant.

USE OF MARGINAL CHARACTERS
This is likely to be more irregular than regular.

If it should be possible for the writers to make it regular, they agreed to do so, though they prefer to have the marginal characters used irregularly.

SYNOPSIS
The writers undertake to submit this, together with a list of characters for booking, at the theme stage, in periods of one, two, three or four weeks.

NATURAL HISTORY AND FOLK LORE
Its place and percentage in the programme should be ten to fifteen per cent.

The writers cannot undertake to attach this to particular characters, but must reserve the right to use it as and when the opportunity arises.

There is a nice touch of irony in a group of men sitting in a city centre pub, solemnly agreeing that life in a fictional, country-pub should not be dominated by alcoholic drinks.

By the end of its first year, the programme had won a regular following of more than six million and the Light Programme bosses were at last ready to concede to Godfrey's dearest wish – his omnibus edition. The special, hour-long compilation of the whole week's happenings in Ambridge finally made its way onto the air in January

Tony Shryane (far right) rehearses (left to right) Harry Oakes (Dan Archer),
Bob Arnold (Tom Forrest), Gwen Berryman (Doris Archer) and Harry
Stubbs (the vicar) for a scene being recorded in Hanbury Church, near
Droitwich, at Christmas 1951.

1952 and was heard on Saturday evenings. It added another three
million regular listeners.

The very success of the programme brought more problems for
the writers. By now, every farmer and farm-worker in the country
seemed to be listening and they were all experts. They sent in suggestions by the bagful, and complaints by the score. Some of the
suggestions were useful – and used; most of the complaints could be
discounted because they invariably arose out of the simple fact that
in the fifties, farming practices differed in different parts of the country. All, however, served to underline Godfrey Baseley's unrelenting
campaign for accuracy and attention to detail, and it led to Tony
Shryane creating the most comprehensive collection of sound effects
available to a single programme. It became a point of honour for
Tony and his recording engineers to use only effects that were exactly
right, and it meant the end of 'pigs grunting', 'cows mooing', 'bird-
song' and similar vaguenesses. Instead, it became 'sow (in pig) grunting', 'sow (hungry) grunting', 'sow (not hungry) grunting' and so

on. The effects were recorded in farms around the Midlands by the engineers but on Tony's strict briefing. On one occasion, Tony needed the sound of a cow having a warble-fly removed from its hide. This is a fairly gruesome business to the urban sensitivities, entailing as it does the use of a stiff scrubbing-brush to scour out the sores caused by the flies, and the recordist decided, for once, to cut corners, producing – by rubbing the brush on a doormat – a very creditable approximation. Tony was on to it instantly and packed the man off to a distant farm to do the job properly. Complete with scrubbing-brush, he arrived at the farm and asked if he could possibly scrub a cow's back. The farmer, who had become used to the ways of The Archers people, simply nodded as if he did not believe the man was mad. In triumph, the engineer returned with the recording and assured Tony that he – personally – had scrubbed the cow. 'Yes,' said Tony, 'but did the cow actually have warble-fly?'

Another major problem stealing up on the programme-makers was the publicity seekers. Almost every organization involved in farming and the countryside (and many that were not) wanted to get in on the act. If The Archers were supposed to be a propaganda exercise, they each wanted their tuppence-worth. A random check of six months' correspondence shows that there were ninety-seven letters to the programme from people with one vested interest or another. Some of them were lucky. If they had information to impart that was thought to be of importance or interest to the audience, they might find it carefully worked into the script. But the majority were unlucky. They were just looking for free publicity and soon found that Mr Baseley and company were far from soft touches. Generations of public-relations men have found the same down through the years. It is also true, of course, that in the early days, the links between the programme and the Ministry of Agriculture were very close, much closer than, for example, would be welcomed by today's BBC executives. At one liaison meeting minuted in 1953, the editor and writers were waited on by no less than sixteen heads of division of the Ministry: 'A discussion followed and a general willingness was expressed by all concerned to co-operate and they offered full facilities at any of their research stations, laboratories and experimental farms.' Even in the face of such Ministry generosity, Godfrey took care to stress 'the necessity of the editor having the final selection of material.'

As well as all the external pressures, the programme continued to suffer internal pains – and again, only because it was so successful. As the storyline progressed, the Ambridge characters developed a kind of reality that made them bigger personalities than even the actors and actresses who played the parts. The producer of a record programme decided to capitalize on that and asked if Dan Archer could present his own show. While most people in Birmingham thought it a jolly good idea, the London hierarchy was unequivocally set against it and a teleprinter message made the position clear: 'Not in favour of the Archers presenting record programmes in character. It would embarrass us with other characters including the Dale family, PC 49, Archie Andrews and Christopher Blaze.' What the message left unexpressed was a growing concern that rather too many people were finding it difficult to believe that Dan and Doris Archer did not actually exist and that the only reason that idyllic Ambridge could not be destroyed by progress was that it could not be found on any map.

But such worries were for later years. Just then the programme was going from strength to strength. In the summer of 1953, it was broadcast on the General Overseas Service of the BBC and was therefore heard by many millions more listeners all over the world. The press mapped the progress with great enthusiasm and never a week went by without an Archers story appearing in one or other of the national papers. At the end of that year, the *Daily Mail* offered it the accolade of 'most entertaining radio programme' in its national radio awards, and this was for a programme originally conceived as an information outlet. (To prove that it was no flash-in-the-pan, the programme collected the same award the following year.)

1953 was also the year that death first crept into discussions about the storyline, with the writers saying that if they were to be realistic, there would have to be a bereavement in Ambridge sooner or later. In fact, it seems from the records that they had already hatched a death plot – to kill off Peggy Archer. But they were foiled before the deed could be done. What happened was that the actress who played Peggy decided she wanted to leave. June Spencer had been with the programme right from the trial run in 1950, but she and her husband felt the time was right for them to begin raising a family. The writers thought the solution was simple: that Peggy should die. But Britain, it seemed, was not yet ready for such a traumatic experience. Because of the importance attached to the programme, discussions of the plan reached the upper echelons of the BBC: first the Light Programme Controller and then the Director of Home Service Broadcasting himself. Finally, after due deliberation, the answer was passed down: 'We both feel that to have a death in The Archers would be a most unfortunate thing and I hope you will therefore be able to resolve your difficulty, if necessary, by employing another actress.' Just how 'unfortunate' a death in the programme might be even those two highly-experienced gentlemen (with every reason to believe that they knew their audience very well) could not have imagined, but were to discover two years later.

June Spencer left (though she came back a year later in a smaller part, returned as Peggy in 1962 and has stayed ever since) and was replaced by Thelma Rogers. This was to be the first of several substitutions made over the years and, somewhat surprisingly, the listeners never seemed to mind overmuch. On this first occasion, there was a little grumbling, but by the time new people had to be found to play Walter Gabriel and Christine Archer, the audience response was warm: 'The "new" Walter (Chris Gittins) . . . is now as loveable an old rogue as ever . . . and, the "new" Christine (Lesley Saweard) . . . fills the role to everyone's satisfaction.'

While the plot was scotched and Peggy's death averted, her 'husband' Jack was having health problems and his condition deteriorated to the point where the doctor warned him that he was heading for a nervous breakdown. It was Franklin Engelmann who first registered the effect of Jack's illness on some of the audience. There were reports, he said, of doctors having surgeries full of Archers fans. They had all decided that their symptoms were the same as Jack's and therefore immediately assumed that they were in for a breakdown. Luckily it was not true – in most cases, at least – but it had Mr Engelmann writing: 'I hope that this doesn't snowball!'

With one in every three of the adult population listening every evening, the programme had the most astonishing grip on the nation. Only two other shows – Wilfred Pickles's *Have a Go* and the almost-institutional *Family Favourites* – had the same size of audience and they, of course, were only once a week. And there can be little doubt that for a great many of the listeners, the line between fact and fiction had become very blurred. This was brought home to Tony Shryane one day when he happened to be on a bus passing the BBC studios in Birmingham. 'That's where The Archers are,' said one lady. 'Really?' replied her friend. 'But how on earth do they get all the cows in there?' And for the actors and actresses who played the parts, life was often confusing. Miss Gwen Berryman (who has played Doris Archer for all of the programme's existence) was always being asked how her husband was keeping and found herself responding completely naturally. Harry Oakes, the first of three Dan Archers, said in an interview that he always answered to the name of 'Dan' as if it were his real name and sometimes did not realize people were talking to him when they called him 'Harry'. He also said that on the days he was to go to the studios, he nearly always found himself putting on his country-style clothes before he was fully

Rehearsing at Broad Street studio in 1954. Standing, Lesley Saweard (Christine Archer) and Gwen Berryman (Doris Archer); seated, left to right, Thelma Rogers (Peggy Archer), Ysanne Churchman (Grace Fairbrother), Joy Davies (Mrs Fairbrother), Pauline Seville (Mrs Perkins) and Tony Shryane.

awake. 'I have to keep reminding myself that I don't have to look like a farmer,' he said.

The one man to keep his feet very firmly on the ground was Godfrey Baseley. He never lost his sense of reality and was determined to keep The Archers exactly what it was – the most professional and successful radio serial. To do that meant ignoring all the plaudits and all the myths that were by now surrounding the programme, and keeping a firm control of the quality of the scripts and the production. In a memo to everyone involved in making the programme, he wrote:

> I have been listening to The Archers very frequently lately and I feel strongly that the quality of the programme is not up to standard. It is very difficult to define where the fault may lie and it seems to me that all members of the team may be at fault to some degree.
>
> I should be very happy if, during the next fortnight, we could

all listen to the episodes and meet and discuss them, and if we agree about the fall in standard, then try to discover some remedy.

Among the replies was this one from the regional programme head, Denis Morris: 'I have just been listening to the week before last's "Archers" and I agree with you that it seems to have changed rather . . . The phoney stage Irish is particularly nauseating, that is a criticism which I have heard from a lot of people, and in the scene where the phoney Irishman and the phoney Italian are talking together, one's patience was almost exhausted.'

The meeting Godfrey called coincided with the broadcast of the one thousandth edition and it was typical of him to be more concerned with resolving problems than with celebration. While he was naturally delighted with all the congratulations (with messages from everybody from the Director-General downwards), he was more concerned with the listeners' reaction. But he need not have worried. The letters received after the one thousandth edition were as complimentary as ever.

However, while The Archers had been moving briskly from success to success, so too had television. The BBC service had been increasing its hours and improving its quality and slowly but all-too-surely, listeners were becoming viewers. It seemed inevitable that the trend would be speeded up when, in 1955, the BBC monopoly in broadcasting was to be broken with the introduction of the new commercial channel. Which brings us to one of the most amazing events in the long history of radio – the death of Grace Archer.

It is difficult to write anything new about the incident, but it is perhaps worth clearing up once and for all the question of whether or not the timing of the death scene with the launching of commercial television was deliberate. A few of the reports at the time hinted at a connection and since then, in all the books published about The Archers, there has been a certain coyness on the part of the programme-makers. They have seemed happy to let people think what they will, to come to their own conclusion. Some, of course, have long thought the nice gentlemen from the BBC had a stroke of luck, while cynics saw in the event the deft touch of a group of very professional communicators. In fact, the cynics were right. The death of Grace, in a stable blaze while she was trying to rescue her horse, was timed to perfection – only minutes before the new channel was opened on the evening of Thursday, 23 September. The result was that it was The Archers that got massive coverage in the press next day. 'Radio fans wept as

Grace Archer "died" ' (*Daily Mirror*); 'Archer fans upset when Grace dies' (*News Chronicle*); 'Why do this to Grace Archer?' (*Daily Express*); 'Millions shocked as Grace dies' (*Daily Herald*); 'Death of BBC serial character' (*The Times*); 'Why Grace Archer died' (*Daily Mail*); 'Listeners sob as Grace Archer "dies" ' (*Daily Sketch*); 'Upset by "death" in The Archers' (*Daily Telegraph*).

That was just the beginning. The stories went on and on. The Sunday papers tried to find new angles and in a full-page feature in the *Sunday Graphic*, Terence Feeley wrote: 'May I respectfully suggest to the women of Britain that the death of poor Grace Archer is something less than a national disaster.' This was under the banner headline, 'Britain's Sob Sisters.' But Mr Feeley was wrong in his assumption that only the womenfolk were upset. The log of telephone calls received at the BBC offices in Birmingham said: 'Men as well as women, were all upset by the Grace Archer tragedy.' As soon as the programme was over calls were coming in. Listeners were broken-hearted, shattered, disgusted and vowing never to listen to this serial again. Some listeners wanted to know who was to be killed off next, why it had been done, and could not Grace, who had endeared herself to so many people, be brought back again? A doctor said he felt a lot of harm had been done and that he was sure the BBC would not dream even of killing Paul Temple! One man wanted to know if Godfrey Baseley had a sadistic streak in him.

On the Friday morning, there was a steady stream of calls: a matron at a hospital had had trouble with some elderly people who listened in before settling down for the night. Several people pointed out an error in saying that the horse returned to the burning stable, and lots of people said the BBC had done its best to kill the programme. There were also many inquiries about Ysanne Churchman who played Grace: was she going to work for the ITA? Was she ill, or having a baby? A works manager at a factory at West Bromwich even said the event had held up production.

That day's calls were mainly groups of people telephoning. Some said they were speaking on behalf of ten or twenty colleagues in their office or works. Calls came from all over the Midland Region, and from Cambridge, Bath and London.

Listeners to the serial were certainly in a revolt. They suggested all kinds of ways of reviving Grace. They accused the BBC of turning 'light entertainment into shocking drama' and 'very bad tactics – presumably because the ITA is opening up this evening'. One listener requested that another wife be found for Philip as soon as possible. Central Services Office Manager reported that at Egton

House (one of the BBC's London offices) the switchboard was completely blocked with telephone calls which came from any part of the country. He requested that, in future, when listeners' reaction was anticipated, his office could be warned so that he could arrange for additional staff to be on duty.

The calls and the newspaper stories rolled on and on for over a month and inevitably the press asked the question 'Who are the guilty men?' It was the *Daily Mail* who first found the right answer:

These are the men who planned the death:

Denis Morris, Head of Midland Region programmes
Rooney Pelletier, Controller, Light Programme
Tony Shryane, Producer
Geoffrey Webb ⎫
⎬ Scriptwriters
Edward J. Mason, ⎭
Godfrey Baseley, founder and editor.

These indeed were the six men who plotted the death. They had met for a normal script conference in June but once the subject of the new commercial television channel was introduced, the whole nature of the meeting changed. The secretary, Valerie Hodgetts (later to become Mrs Shryane), was told not to duplicate and distribute minutes as she had always done up to then. Everyone was then sworn to secrecy – which was not surprising with death on the agenda, because that was what had been unanimously agreed would have the biggest impact. Next came a discussion about who should be the victim and a shortlist was drawn up – Christine Archer, Carol Grey (later to become Mrs Tregorran) and the newly-wed Grace Archer. It is not clear who voted for whom, but in the end it was Grace who was destined to be the sacrificial lamb. Then someone pointed out that because of her independent nature, Grace was not one of the best-loved characters. It seemed that after her marriage to Philip Archer, she had upset him and many of the audience by declaring that she had no intention of starting a family. So, before further talk about the death, it was agreed that Grace should change her mind and become pregnant (this was actually in the script just two weeks before the death) and thus endear herself to all the listeners. If that sounds a little cold-blooded, the ensuing comments showed commendable concern for the audience. Grace should die after a miscarriage, said someone. No, no, that would upset every expectant mother in the land. Grace should die in a road accident. No, that would frighten everybody whose wife was out in her car at the time. How about her dying in a stable fire, then? Yes, that was it – and if she first escaped the flames and then rushed back into the blazing stables to try to save her horse, would not that be a fitting end for a heroine?

With the conspiracy concluded, the problem then became one of security. Any leak and the whole plan would collapse. No minutes were circulated and no further discussion was to take place until the very day of the event. By way of camouflage, it was agreed that during the appropriate week an experiment on topicality should be conducted. This meant that instead of writing the scripts in advance, Ted Mason and Geoffrey Webb would try doing it on the day of the broadcast so that they could work in as many up-to-date references as possible. For good measure, it was also decided that this set of programmes be made in London. It all worked like a charm. Outside the seven who had been at the meeting, no one guessed that anything was afoot. The cast, who had usually had their scripts the previous week, were quite happy with the story Tony Shryane spun about the topical try-out.

On the day itself, the BBC publicity office was told that The Archers that evening would be 'quite interesting' and it might be a good idea to invite the press in for a preview. This was done, and such was the general appeal of the programme that all of the national daily papers were represented at about five o'clock (deliberately too late for that day's evening papers) when the episode was recorded. As the final scene ended, with Phil saying, 'She's dead,' there was a stunned silence. The allegedly hard-bitten newsmen did not quite believe what they had just heard and anyway, there was no closing music so there was probably some kind of mix-up. They sat around uncertainly. They had never faced death quite like this before. Then all hell broke loose, with reporters dashing everywhere, trying to speak to the cast, the writers, the producer and the editor all at the same time. In the confusion, one young journalist, who had obviously seen too many films about his trade, snatched the nearest telephone, dialled his office and was demanding his newsdesk to tell them about a scoop, only to discover it was a dummy phone used as a studio prop. In the end, he and all the others found real telephones and told their stories, but not before the Light Programme listeners had heard it themselves that evening. In the days that followed, the BBC estimated that some fifteen thousand letters of protest were received – it was impossible to count the number of telephone calls – and a pair of coffin-handles and brass plates were delivered to the Birmingham studios. For fear that they would be inundated with flowers, it was decided that 'the funeral' would not be held within the programme.

It might be hard to believe after all that, but life for the

programme people did go on as normal. They continued to make
programmes – and to resist suggestions that they deemed unsuitable
– from whatever source:

> At his meeting with Regional Controllers last week, DG raised
> the question of broadcasts on industry, and there was a reference
> to the proposed industrial serial. DG said in passing that there
> was something tempting about inserting an industrial ingredient
> into The Archers, although this obviously had its dangers.
>
> I am inclined to suggest that it would be worth while at your
> next editorial meeting to take, at any rate, a first look at this
> possibility. One way of bringing in an industrial element would
> be for Fairbrother to open a factory in Ambridge. One would
> envisage the industrial strand as secondary to the country strand,
> although from time to time it might come into the centre of the
> picture. Whether it could be done without jeopardizing the
> essential quality of the programme would be a matter for careful
> thought, but the programme has already digested so much that it
> might conceivably take industrial matters in its stride.

The writers thought such a development *would* jeopardize the quality
of the programme, not to say the quality of life in the rural community. Ambridge was spared the factory.

Meanwhile, overseas interest in The Archers was increasing.
Someone from the South Africa Broadcasting Corporation (who said
Grace's death had been widely reported there) asked about the possibility of having the scripts translated into Afrikaans. It was Hugh
Carleton Greene (then Controller, Overseas Service, but later Director-General) who knocked that idea on the head: 'We cannot imagine
how it would be possible to adapt and produce in South Africa a
programme which is closely related to local English village life, agricultural methods, social conventions, weather and current events,
and still retain enough of the original to justify the use of its title. In
fact, the whole idea seems quite fantastic and has clearly not been
properly thought out in all its implications.'

The Americans were next to show interest in the programme and
a misunderstanding over exactly what they wanted threatened an
international incident. The initial inquiry was from the Department
of Agriculture in Washington and they were told very smartly that
they could not have tapes for trial broadcasting. Then it became clear
that all they wanted was to listen and analyse some episodes, with a
view to devising a similar kind of programme for US farmers. Some
BBC executives were still not happy until a liaison officer warned
that under British law there was no copyright protection of pro-

The Archers in the studio, 1955. Left to right, Norman Painting (Philip),
Gwen Berryman (Doris), Lesley Saweard (Christine) and Harry Oakes
(Dan).

gramme ideas, and he added: 'Since the US embassy here could quite
easily get all that they really needed by merely listening to the programme, I feel that in the interests of good relations with the Americans (from whom we get a great deal in various ways), we might as
well give with a good grace what could easily be taken from us
against our will.'

It seemed as if the whole world was interested in the everyday
story of countryfolk. The regional head of programmes visited
Vienna and was immediately asked why the programme could not
be broadcast on the European Service. He took the idea up but was
told: 'I am afraid this is quite impracticable for a number of reasons.
For one thing, the scripts would need to be entirely re-written to
enable them to be fitted in to our periods, and to allow sufficient
time for linguistic explanation.' This seems a pity. It would have
been a joy to hear how Walter Gabriel's 'Me old pal, me old beauty'
was explained to the European listeners.

Commercial radio in Australia also wanted to buy the programme
but as it was already being heard down-under on the BBC's own

General Overseas Service, another polite refusal was penned. In fact, there were few corners of the world that could not hear the programme. Apart from Australia and New Zealand, the places mentioned on a check-list in 1956 were East Africa, Arabia, Egypt, Israel, Jordan, Lebanon, Sudan, Syria, Turkey, West Africa, Malta, Greece, Italy, Gibraltar, Japan, North China, North-West Pacific, South-East Asia, India, Pakistan and Ceylon. Around the same time, Tony Shryane received a note from an engineering colleage in Leeds: 'I don't know if you could use this information or not, but among other people who are devoted to The Archers is the crew of the *Rinovia*, a fishing trawler. The skipper, Mr Karl Sigurdsson, is an Icelander, and it is as much as his wireless operator's life is worth to fail to provide his 'Archers'. Even the trawl has to wait. The bond between 'ploughing the deep', 'harvesting the sea' (and other platitudinous expressions) is extremely strong.'

While the programme was being so avidly listened to on the high seas, Godfrey Baseley and the writers were themselves getting into deep water with one of their story-lines. They planned that Dan Archer should be one of Britain's farmers then changing over from a dairy Shorthorn herd to Friesians, the breed imported originally from Holland. The reason for the change was to do with the milk yield and Dan's involvement was a good example of the programme being up-to-date in reflecting what was happening in agriculture. However, Godfrey happened to mention the idea to the secretary of the Shorthorn Society and from then on the plan went awry, with the BBC's Director-General (then Sir Ian Jacob) finally becoming involved. In a series of letters, most of which were very technical, the Society expressed strong fears that Dan Archer's change-over to Friesians could have 'serious implications' for the British Shorthorn. In the end, the BBC had to concede that the programme's strength – its influence on an enormous audience – was also its weakness in this kind of argument. There was no doubt that what Dan Archer did one day, others were quite likely to follow the next day. The plan was shelved and the Shorthorns were saved to live on at Brookfield Farm, at least for the time being.

It was not only the agriculturists who were concerned that the undoubtedly potent influence of the programme could be misdirected. One scene between the rather flighty Irish girl, Rita Flynn (she was the assistant in Doughy Hood's bakery shop), and one of the village lads aroused many people's indignation. One anxious lady wrote, 'The Archers used to be for family listening but recently it has become disgusting. What with Rita Flynn, etc.' Another said, 'It is nothing but a lot of suggestiveness instead of a story of country life.' At this distance, it is all too easy to discount such comments by assuming the writers must have been unusually prim, because the offending scene now seems innocuous enough. But then one finds this memo from a very senior executive: 'I am getting a good many complaints – as in the attached copy letter – about the sexiness of The Archers these days and I hear from my son in the Regular Army in Germany that it is now eagerly listened to in the Mess to see in what shape sex will rear its ugly head each night.'

It is hard to believe now that it was The Archers that should be the troops' comforter in post-war Germany. But it was, of course, still several years before the permissiveness of the Swinging Sixties.

Not long after, a second and more serious fall from grace occurred and again it was because of a hint of sex, this time in a scene between the young Carol Grey and Toby Stobeman. One letter reached the Director-General: 'I think it is disgraceful that the BBC should permit an episode in The Archers with implied immorality between "Toby Stobeman" and "Carol Grey" which I heard in the omnibus edition this morning. I hope you heard it and take the same view and will take such action as will make a re-occurrence impossible. It has debased the "Archer" programmes which, so far as I have heard them, have always been good, wholesome and helpful to country people in portraying agricultural and rural life.'

To that and others, the BBC responded with an apology that explained: 'A high proportion of fictional work in printed form, on the stage, cinema and radio inevitably is concerned with illicit love affairs. There is not, however, any intention of exploiting such a subject in The Archers. I am sorry that the omnibus edition to which you listened gave you that impression. On looking at the scripts I have come to the conclusion that the scene you complain of was faded out at an injudicious moment in its development, and the attention of those concerned is being drawn to the matter.' What the public did not know, however, was just how seriously the BBC hierarchy viewed the situation. The production team really were told in no uncertain terms that they had gone astray. One memo said, 'I cannot myself remember any period when The Archers has been less than true to itself with a cheap storyline and hardly any farming.' A second picked up the point about where the scene was faded out. 'It was faded out at a moment and after such scenes of heavy breathing and what you will, that could only lead one to suppose that Miss Grey had forgotten her mother's good advice – a supposition more than confirmed in the episode covering the following day, during which Miss Grey did a good deal more sighing of a retrospective and reflective character, and again left the more worldly listener in no doubt as to what had happened on the sofa.'

At the time that row was going on, there was also a fair amount of violence in the programme, with Tom Forrest actually being sent to jail to await trial for shooting and killing a poacher. Much concern was expressed about Tom's predicament and great relief when he was acquitted, but it appears there was not a single complaint about the violence. However, the programme-makers did respond to the strictness about sex and innuendo. Godfrey Baseley conceded that the episodes complained of were 'on the whole a little cheap' and he wrote to Ted Mason and Geoff Webb: 'I am sure you will be the first to agree with me that we must never allow this label to be attached to the programme.' It is hardly surprising that the idea of introducing a story about illegitimacy was discussed only briefly at the next script conference and then quietly disappeared from subsequent minutes of meetings. Instead, everyone concentrated on the forthcoming wedding of Phil (now recovered from the trauma of Grace's death) and Jill, and in making sure that the courtship of Tom Forrest and Pru was conducted quietly and with decorum. This was the everyday story of country folk that the listeners wanted to hear. And without sex to worry about, senior executives could turn their attention once more to scrutinizing the general quality of the programme. For example:

> I found the cricket match exceedingly unconvincing. The applause was far too smooth and unlike any applause I have ever heard in a village cricket match. A lot of the remarks creaked. The time it took Uncle Tom to get from the wicket when he was dismissed to the pavilion suggested that the game was played at the Oval or an even larger ground and the statement towards the end of the game by one of the Ambridge side that he was sure they were going to win as they only needed another twenty-five (or thirty-five?) with three wickets to go shows that the scriptwriters are not aware of what usually happens in village cricket.

Nowadays, much of these comments would be regarded as nit-picking, but it was, in fact, simple professionalism from a hierarchy that was fully aware of the value of its property. Just how valuable was The Archers can be seen not just in the size of its audience – peaking at twenty million in 1955 – but also in the constant coverage it got in the press; in the staggering number of personal appearances made by the actors and actresses (always as the characters they played); and by the constant attempts of commercial interests to jump on the bandwagon, including the makers of advertisements for television.

Tony Shryane gives notes to the cast, 1955. Back row, Leslie Bowmar, Norman Painting, Harry Oakes, Denis Folwell. Front row, Joy Davies, Anne Cullen, Lesley Saweard, Gwen Berryman, Leslie Dunn.

It was not only commercial television, however, that wanted to use the influence of The Archers. The BBC's own television service asked for help in its campaign to increase the sale of television sets and thus the number of viewers. Godfrey Baseley's initial response was blunt. He thought (rightly as it turned out) that every new set represented a potentially-lost listener and he, understandably, saw no reason to damage his own prospects. Sadly, he was persuaded to act against his better judgement. Dan Archer did buy a television set for Brookfield Farm and we now know that millions followed his example in subsequent years. In a way, it was the thin edge of the wedge that would eventually break the dominance of radio in the British home and cause a steady shrinkage of the audience for the programme itself. In fact, during 1957, the daily figures for The Archers had dropped by nearly a million and although this was offset by an increase of just over a million for the week-end omnibus edition, it was clear that television was a potent force to be reckoned with. And The Archers' team started reckoning in the only way that mattered. The minutes of the next script-conference noted: 'A strong story-line is planned for the summer, instead of the usual pattern of small uneventful plots.' Those were the days before transistors and car-radios, so when people went out-of-doors to enjoy the summer sunshine, they could not listen in even if they had wanted to, which meant it was a good time for the writers to recharge their own batteries. But in the face of the growing competition and with their two-thousandth episode coming up in September, the summer of 1958 was different for The Archers. New stories included serious financial problems for Dan Archer, and even the possibility that rising costs would force him and Doris to give up Brookfield Farm. Jill's pregnancy would proceed normally, but cracks would begin to show in the marriage of Christine and Paul Johnson. Still very conscious of the audience's sensitiveness, it was stressed that divorce should not be mentioned, and when someone suggested that it could be discovered that Mr Fairbrother was illegitimate, it was decreed that this was 'rather distasteful'.

The broadcast of the programme's two-thousandth episode was marked in the story by the wedding of Tom Forrest and Pru Harris, and in reality by a rather special Harvest Home evening at the Warwickshire farm of Mr Clyde Higgs, Chairman of the BBC's agricultural advisory committee. As is often the case on anniversaries, the two writers, Geoff Webb and Ted Mason, felt the need to ponder the future and at the meeting on the day of the celebrations, they stressed the importance of attracting new, younger listeners. Towards that end, they said they would like to 'reflect in the programme the real problems of the teenager of today, the peacock-like attitude towards clothes, the perpetual fight against adults, a desire to show independence and the complete aimlessness and lack of ambition.' They were given the go-ahead 'as long as the treatment was woven into the pattern . . . and that the impression was not given that this was typical of the whole generation of teenagers.' This concern for reflecting contemporary life at all levels has always stood The Archers in good stead and it is today still one of the cornerstones of the programme's policy.

The publicity associated with The Archers had always been carefully orchestrated, but for the two-thousandth episode, Kenneth Bird, the regional publicity officer, really excelled himself. He had suggested publishing a special edition of *The Borchester Echo*, the local paper which, in the story, covered the Ambridge area. He envisaged a sixteen-page paper that would include articles by those closely-identified with the programme – Ted Mason, Geoff Webb, Godfrey Baseley, Tony Shryane, the artistes who played Dan, Doris and Walter Gabriel – plus other features from a crossword puzzle to a children's competition. With a selling price of sixpence, Kenneth Bird estimated that they could sell as many as a quarter of a million copies. He was hopelessly wrong – the eventual sale was well over a million.

This did much to restore confidence among the programme staff and, no doubt, helped them to cope with the general strain of maintaining their own high standards. Simply keeping the programme going demanded consistent and total commitment to The Archers, so much so that anyone being so extravagant as to have a holiday, could throw the whole system out of synchronization. In fact, it was due to the incredible organization of Tony Shryane, as producer, that over the years, The Archers gained the highest reputation both for its use of resources and for always being within its limited budget. He created a blueprint for script control, casting, costing and production that is still used today. This includes a limitation of the number of artistes that can be used in each episode, a factor which can sometimes be restricting for the script-writers, as can be seen in this exchange of memos:

> You may remember I wrote about three weeks ago to Ted Mason saying that there was a good deal of evidence of recent Archers' scripts being depressing and sordid. He has now replied saying that he feels that the story line, as agreed at the Script Conference, is a bit of a depressing one, and that he is all in favour of livening the programmes up and putting more gaiety and humour into them. He is worried about the 'dreadful sameness' of the episodes, which he says is due to the restriction of using only three extra characters in each one, so, whatever the story, it is the same old voices telling it. Would you look into this and see if you can suggest any other economies which would enable us to have another voice or two?

It was again Tony Shryane who did look into it.

> I agree with Ted Mason that it is difficult to get very much variety into The Archers with the authors being restricted to using only three extra characters per episode. If, however, more characters are used, this would mean an over-spending of our present allowance. I would like to suggest a possible way of using extra characters which could be discussed at the next script conference.

Tony's possible way involved using members of the BBC Repertory in London. The metropolitan executives could not decide whether or not that was another regional ploy, but Tony got the money he needed for the additional characters without further argument.

It was not just a matter of logistics that had been giving the writers problems. It was also the simple fact that they had been in constant harness for more than eight years and had written more than two thousand scripts, covering almost every permutation of rural life (and of course, before The Archers, both had worked for several years on *Dick Barton*). It was inevitable that, from time to time, they would have difficulty finding new stories – or fresh ways of treating old stories – and in keeping the scripts bright and sparkling. Both were now calling on all their reserves as experienced hands at the soap-opera game and this had its advantages, because they turned more and more to what was happening in the countryside on a day-to-day basis, with the result that the programme was more up-to-date than ever. But it meant they also rushed headlong into trouble with one section of the community. The danger signal came in a news story issued by the Press Association to every newspaper in the country.

The Executive Committee of the league against cruel sports today decided to protest to the Director-General of the BBC about 'the introduction of propaganda in favour of foxhunting' into The Archers programme. For several nights past this feature has gone out of its way to favour foxhunting and eulogize it as a country sport, instead of revealing it as despicable cruelty. We call on you to instruct the script-writers of this feature to introduce something which will show foxes as the pest to farmers that they really are, and so put foxes and foxhunting in their proper perspective in rural life.

The script-writers never did get instructions, but they did continue to get letters, some of them quite wild: 'Remarks about killing a chicken and having "a good day with the guns" were positively revolting . . . It may interest you to know that the British Union against Vivisection, the League against Cruel Sports and the RSPCA have all received numerous complaints about this disgusting programme . . . undoubtedly the broadcasting authorities must, in the end, take some account of public opinion.' This was, perhaps, a sour note on which to end the fifties, but it showed without any shadow of doubt that nine years had not irremediably blunted the writers' pens, and also that the great British public were still avidly listening to what was going on in Ambridge.

CHAPTER 2

The Ambridge Chronicles 1950–9

compiled by William Smethurst,
Producer of The Archers

They must always have been there, of course. Farming, quarrelling, helping each other, misunderstanding each other, enjoying the countryside, and having an abnormally large number of accidents. It was just that before the wireless was invented people could not hear them, and before 1951 the true potential of the wireless was not fully realized.

But they must have been there – in that far-from-sleepy English village, out beyond the Vale of Evesham, somewhere on the borders of Worcestershire, Warwickshire and Gloucestershire, where on 25 August 1896, the infant Walter Gabriel first gave breath, closely followed six weeks later by the first cry of baby Daniel Archer.

Walter and Daniel, and a few years later the Forrest children Doris and Tom – roses that would blush unseen for over fifty years, wasting their fragrance on the unharnessed airwaves. Little Doris in her pinafore and Tom in his knickerbockers out on the school treat – we know about that because they have talked about it since. Then Tom getting a job as 'the lad' on Squire Lawson-Hope's estate, and Doris going into service with Lettie Lawson-Hope. Daniel Archer – a steady, respectful young man of twenty-one – getting one of the Squire's smaller farms to run, and walking out with Doris in 1918. They were married two years later, on 17 December 1920, and two years later to the day their first child, Jack, was born.

The twenties were hard times on the land, and perhaps economic hardship accounts for the delay of six years before a second son, Philip, was born. Three years later, on 21 December 1931, Doris gave birth to a daughter, Christine.

What episodes were missed in those days! How many times must Jack nearly have been drowned in the village pond, Christine nearly have been trampled to death by horses, and Philip nearly have succumbed to some childhood ailment! How many times must Daniel have fallen badly in his barn, hammered his fingers, and been kicked by cows – for it has become clear since that he is particularly subject to such misfortunes.

The very act of farming was a risky, nail-biting affair, harvests really were make or break. Today God sends the sun and rain, and the government sends the subsidy, but it was not until 1936 that Daniel sat down at the scrubbed table in the kitchen at Brookfield and puzzled over his first government grant form. Then he went out, harnessed up Blossom and Boxer, and put an extra twenty acres to the plough. Brookfield wheat would help defeat the U-boats, and Dan would receive subsidies, and fill in forms, for the rest of his working life.

And so the saga continued . . . Young Philip winning a place at Borchester Grammar School, the first Archer to receive a full secondary education. Christine following his example with a scholarship, and getting her HSC with distinction in biology and a credit in chemistry. Jack serving in the army, and meeting a pretty young ATS girl, Peggy Perkins, who said she was a socialist. And for Daniel and Doris (she called him Daniel at first, and he called her 'mother'), there was the worry of running Brookfield. Would farming decline, as it had after the First World War? Ought they to buy a tractor, and put Blossom and Boxer out to grass?

By New Year's Eve 1950, however, when the Archer family met for their traditional party in the parlour of Brookfield Farm, it must have seemed to Daniel and Doris that the great events of their lives were over. The subsidies were flowing as steadily as ever, their children were grown up, and they could settle into a comfortable, ripe middle-age. True, Jack was still a worry – he had married Peggy Perkins, but could only scratch a living on a smallholding in the village; and Christine, an outside milk sampler at the Ministry of Agriculture, was a bit flighty and always chasing after unsuitable men. But Philip was as steady as a rock. He was already, at twenty-two, farm manager for Mr Fairbrother, earning £1 a week more than the national weekly average, and he was going around with Fairbrother's daughter, Grace, who everybody said was a nice young girl.

Doris did not dare be too hopeful, however, because Grace was also being pursued by Lieutenant Alan Carey, a tanks officer who was wounded in Korea and was having a hard time adjusting to peacetime life. But on New Year's Eve, 1950, Grace came with Phil to the party at Brookfield – a private, family affair, like so many family gatherings throughout the country.

It was not until the next day, 1 January 1951, that the whole wide world started to listen in.

1951

At Brookfield, Dan reluctantly decided to buy a tractor. He put Blossom out to grass and sold his other shire horse, Boxer, to Walter Gabriel. His shorthorn dairy herd became attested, giving him an extra fourpence a gallon for his milk.

Phil was in love with his employer's daughter, Grace Fairbrother, but she was fascinated by Lt Alan Carey, a 24-year-old guest of Squire Lawson-Hope, who had been badly shot up in Korea and was now neurotic, bitter and anti-social. Grace found she could help him to regain his confidence in life, and Phil thought himself better off

The Archer family at breakfast.

with Jane Maxwell, a tall, willowy blonde with blue eyes. He engaged her to look after the Fairbrother's poultry scheme. Grace was furious when she saw Phil and Jane in the woods on a rabbiting party, and later found Jane in Phil's arms late at night in the farm office. Phil ran after Grace, jumped on the running board of her car, hit his head on a tree branch, and was knocked out. Then Lt Carey went off to the Lake District, and Grace proposed to Phil. But he told her he was too fond of Jane Maxwell.

The major event in Ambridge this year was the discovery of iron-stone deposits on Fairbrother's land – three million tons of it spread over one hundred acres. Fairbrother wanted to develop the site, and called in a mineralogist, Keith Latimer, who began test drillings and became friendly with Christine Archer (who was already friendly with Dick Raymond, reporter on the *Borchester Echo*).

Returning home from watching *Tilly of Bloomsbury* in Borchester one night, Keith Latimer and Christine saw a saboteur running away from Latimer's drilling equipment, and found the diamond 'bit' was missing. Then, when reporter Dick Raymond was having tea at Brookfield, he phoned his office and accidentally overheard two saboteurs planning another attempt on the drill. Dick, Phil and Keith Latimer decided to wait for the saboteurs, and fought with them.

Peggy Archer gave birth to a son, Anthony William Daniel, on 16 February, and Peggy's mother moved to Ambridge bringing a great deal of furniture with her. Known ever afterwards as Mrs P, she was described as a sharp-featured, black-coated woman, who always moaned when she was feeling happy.

Mrs P lodged in a cottage with Peggy's cousin, Bill Slater, a Londoner who suffered from asthma and had been advised to move to the country. He was given a job at Brookfield, but Dan found him a bad worker. In the autumn he got into a fight outside The Bull, hit his head, and died. Dick Raymond found Latimer's diamond 'bit' in Mrs P's coalshed – Slater was obviously the saboteur.

It was a fine summer. Dan was made vice-president of the tennis club, and when he and Doris went on holiday to Aberystwyth, Christine and Phil gave a party for the cricket club at Brookfield. Doris revealed that Dan hated pyjamas and always wore a nightshirt.

Walter Gabriel was proud when he heard that his only son, Nelson, had been promoted to corporal in the RAF (where he was doing national service). To his further delight, Walter heard he had been left a partnership in a sheep farm and goldmine in Australia by his Uncle Nat. He later found that the sheep farm and goldmine were useless. He cheered up, however, when Dick Raymond interviewed him about his experiences in the Home Guard, and how he once shot a scarecrow in mistake for an enemy parachutist. Walter said they'd be wanting him back now the Home Guard was being reformed.

In the autumn, Dan was disappointed by his sugar beet. The factory complained about dirt tare and said the beet had not been properly topped. In November he received another complaint, from the dairy, who said that Brookfield milk was low on butterfat content. Dan realized he had been feeding too many beet tops to the cows.

The ironstone scheme was rejected after a public inquiry, and Fairbrother took Grace away from Ambridge saying they would never come back. Jack Archer was offered a partnership in a 120 acre farm in Cornwall by his wartime friend Barney Lee. Doris was reluctant to see him leave Ambridge, particularly as she was so fond of her grandchildren, six-year old Jennifer, four-year old Lilian, and Anthony William Daniel who was not yet one.

1952

Dan sold his six cows giving low-fat-content milk, and bought two high quality Shorthorns for one hundred guineas each. Amber gained second prize, best of all breeds, at the Borchester Show.

Doris became upset when she found a page of a letter in a library book which seemed to infer that Christine's boyfriend, reporter Dick Raymond, had deserted a wife and two children. Happily it turned out to be a case of mistaken identity.

Christine's romance, however, was not to last the year out. She became friendly with a Lady Hyleberrow, a strange woman who called Christine 'Felicity' (the name of her daughter who had disappeared). Lady Hyleberrow was shocked to find that Christine went around with boys, and proposed taking her as her companion on a trip to Ethiopia. But Dan and Doris opposed the idea strongly, and Dan offered Christine a job at Brookfield, looking after the poultry. Dick Raymond also got fed up, accepted a job as junior correspondent for South East Asia on a national newspaper and went off to Malaya.

Phil again started going out with Grace, who had returned with her father from London. Jane Maxwell left, and Grace began looking after the poultry at Coombe Farm.

Peggy and Jack moved to Cornwall in the spring, and Dan bought their smallholding for £1,300. In the summer, however, they returned because Barney Lee had started to get too fond of Peggy. They decided to apply for the licence of The Bull, and this was given to them later in the year. By then, however, Peggy was in Felpersham Isolation Hospital with diphtheria.

Phil also had medical problems. Against all advice, he tried to plough the top field on Lakey Hill, and when the tractor stalled he hit his head on the exhaust and developed eye trouble. He had an operation, which was successful. Grace visited him in hospital, but their romance seemed to be making little progress. Phil told her he would like her as his future wife, but had to make £2,000 first. He was shattered when Grace said she had no intention of waiting five years. Phil sold his motor bike for £80 and started saving hard.

There was a warm, dry summer this year – twenty-seven days without rain in July in the Ambridge area. Hay was good at Brookfield, and the winter wheat in Five Acre Field was looking fine when a jet plane crashed on it in August.

Doris was astonished and flattered when Mrs Lawson-Hope and Mrs Fairbrother proposed to nominate her as president of Ambridge Women's Institute – but was reduced to tears when people started accusing her of trying to buy votes by giving away bottles of preserved fruit.

Reggie Trentham, a keen rider at point-to-points and director of Grey Gables Country Club, accused Irish thriller-writer Mike Daly, MC, (who had bought Blossom Hill Cottage as a rural retreat) of really being Major John Smith of the Army Pay Corps, who was cashiered for embezzling funds. Daly dismissed the charge as nonsense, but Reggie Trentham turned up at Blossom Hill Cottage one day with a girl, Valerie Grayson, who had been Major John Smith's girl friend. Mike and Valerie then told the truth: Mike Daly, MC, had been in Dachau concentration camp, and the British authorities had arranged his escape by getting a pro-British German officer to certify him as being dead. Returning to England he had been cashiered from the Army Pay Corps as Major John Smith to arouse the interest of enemy agents, and Valerie Grayson, also a secret service agent, had been his fiancée for convenience. Reggie Trentham accepted the explanation, and soon after married Valerie Grayson.

At Christmas, Dan sold his turkeys to the Imperial Hotel in Borchester, and bought a horse called Midnight from Reggie Trentham. He gave it to Christine for her birthday.

Walter Gabriel tried to make a television set for Mrs P but failed.

1953

Coronation year, and the people of Ambridge spent a lot of time planning bonfires and celebrations. To mark the new age Dan planned to grow lucerne for the first time, and to try his hand at making silage. In May there was an outbreak of swine-fever at the piggery.

During the spring it looked as if Phil were going to lose Grace to the Squire's nephew, Clive Lawson-Hope, who had come to Ambridge to try and put his uncle's estate on a sound financial footing. Clive took Grace to the pictures, and kissed her in the car on the way home. He said it was his firm intention to marry her. Grace asked for time to think, and she was still thinking several weeks later when Clive told her he had changed his mind and did not want to get married.

Peggy came out of hospital, and was distressed to hear rumours about Jack and the Ambridge schoolmistress, Elsie Catcher, who had been helping with the children while Peggy was ill. Jack dismissed the rumours as nonsense. Although he was now landlord of The Bull, he insisted on doing farming work in the area. Peggy said he had a grass-

Clive Lawson-Hope (Leslie Parker), right, and Philip Archer (Norman Painting), left, locked in rivalry over Grace Fairbrother (Ysanne Churchman).

hopper mind. She was forced to take over as licensee of The Bull when the brewery complained about the way it was being run.

Walter Gabriel decided to hold a coronation party at his farm, and had the building wired for Mrs P's television set, which she bought from a Borchester store. He confided to Jack that he was growing very fond of Mrs P – and his affection seemed to be returned when Mrs P gave up a ticket to watch the Coronation in London so that she could attend his party.

On Coronation Eve, Phil and Grace stayed roasting potatoes on the bonfire on Lakey Hill until four o'clock in the morning. She told him she was going to go to Ireland for a year and train in horse management. He told her she was crazy, and they quarrelled bitterly at her farewell party at the Country Club. Mrs P offered to lend Phil some money, so that he could speed up his new pig breeding scheme and afford to marry Grace straight away.

All in all it was a bad year for Walter Gabriel. He was stunned when half his flock were killed and injured by dogs in the spring, and in the summer he had to be rushed to Southampton by police car when Nelson was taken seriously ill and admitted to an RAF hospital. Walter did not return for several weeks, and when he did he was very weak after giving blood to Nelson. Mrs P looked after his orphan lambs in the spring, and gave him nourishing food in the summer.

Tom Forrest also had a bad time. After being hurt in a fight with a poacher, a fire broke out in the Squire's wood and Tom had to evacuate his cottage and move his dogs to Brookfield.

In the autumn, a mysterious figure appeared on the Ambridge scene. A 'bearded young wanderer with a green caravan' was discovered on Heydon Berrow, and was at first regarded with deep suspicion. Tom thought he was the poacher he fought with in the woods, and Christine suspected him of stealing one of her horses. But he was cleared when he went to a gypsy site and forced the gypsies who had taken Christine's horse to give it back. Jack, however, remained wary, and accused him of stealing the Christmas Club money from The Bull.

The young wanderer remained a mystery until Ann Trentham, a pretty young cousin of Reggie Trentham, came to stay at the Country Club. She recognized him as John Tregorran, a lecturer at her university who had won £12,000 on the football pools.

In the late autumn, Squire Lawson-Hope was forced to sell Coombe Farm to Fairbrother, and Dan transferred his pullets from free range to deep litter.

At Christmas, Walter Gabriel allowed John Tregorran to put his

caravan in his rick yard, and a few days later a fire broke out and the
caravan was extensively damaged. John Tregorran was convinced
that the fire was started by gypsies.

1954

There was a bitter winter and a cold spring, and heavy rain throughout the summer ruined the haymaking in Ambridge and delayed the
corn harvest. Dan was relieved to find that yields were above average.

In the spring, Christine became romantically involved with the
Squire's nephew, Clive Lawson-Hope. Phil objected to her friendship
– partly because Clive had recently been chasing after Grace, and
partly because of the unscrupulous way he was trying to hound Walter Gabriel out of his forty-acre farm. Squire Lawson-Hope objected
because Christine was the daughter of one of his tenant farmers. In
March, however, Clive proposed to Christine, having been left a
farm in Kenya by his Uncle Percy. Christine turned him down, and
he went off to Africa alone.

Dan decided to sell the smallholding, and it was bought by a
smartly-dressed young lady from Surrey called Carol Grey, who said
she had plans to start up a market garden. Carol had no sooner
arrived in the village than she drove round a bend and knocked John
Tregorran off his scooter.

In early summer, a young and rather dashing horse-owner called
Paul Johnson saw Christine out riding, and approached Dan to ask
his permission for Christine to ride for him at a two-day show at
Belverston. After discussing the matter with Doris, Dan agreed to
her going away for the two days.

Jack was away from Ambridge for four months, after Peggy insisted that he see a doctor because of his erratic behaviour and fits of ill
temper. The doctor arranged for him to enter the county hospital for
nervous and mental disorders as a voluntary patient.

Dan and Doris received a second shock when the Squire called and
told them he was going to sell the estate. He said it was a hard
decision – the Lawson-Hopes and their tenant families had been
bound together for generations. There was a Blower with the Lawson-Hopes at Sedgemoor, an Archer at Waterloo, and a Gabriel was
his father's batman at Vimy Ridge. Three dozen men of the village
were in the yeomanry regiment which the Squire commanded in the
last war. Dan was offered first option to buy Brookfield, and after
several days of worry he managed to raise enough money.

Much of the estate – including Walter Gabriel's farm – was offered
to Fairbrother. Walter was confident that he would not be evicted,

and offered John Tregorran a job as his right-hand man, with a fair living wage and a Christian roof over his head. John, however, discovered that Walter was only interested in his pools fortune, and decided to leave Ambridge altogether. On the way out of the village he was attacked by gypsies, and decided to stay after all.

In Phil's life, everything was going well. He was busy building up a Hereford herd at Coombe Farm, and moved his pig breeding scheme there in the summer. Grace sent him a set of fishing rods for his birthday, and then a telegram to say she was coming home. They quarrelled at her welcome-home party (he thought she was flirting with Paul Johnson), then he proposed to her, and she said 'yes'. Dan and Doris breathed a sigh of relief. Doris said she had thought it would never happen. Fairbrother offered to rent them Coombe Farmhouse for a rent of one pound a week.

Mike Daly, MC, the Irish thriller-writer and secret-service agent, bought seventy acres of woodland from the Squire, then asked Valerie Trentham, his former aide in the Secret Service if she would join him on 'special work'. Valerie refused. A few days later a woman called Baroness Czorva arrived and told Mike a certain party was expecting to see him. Mike left the village with her.

Romance was in the Ambridge air that autumn. John Tregorran found Christine alone at Brookfield and kissed her, and a few weeks later he suddenly proposed to Carol Grey. She did not reply.

1955

In January, Dan sent half a ton of hay to distressed farmers in flood areas, and reluctantly decided to sell Blossom. Haymaking in June was still largely unmechanized at Brookfield, and involved Dan, Len, Simon, and Walter; with Jack, John Tregorran and PC Bryden helping. Myxomatosis reached Ambridge, but did not stop the Squire holding a final shoot for his former tenants and his friends. He reassured Tom about his future on the estate now Fairbrother was taking over, and gave him a one pound a week pension for the rest of his life.

It was a hectic time at Brookfield. Phil and Grace were due to be married on Easter Monday, but Phil tried to change the date after Jack pointed out the tax advantages of marrying sooner. Grace met the suggestion with an icy refusal.

Christine was becoming increasingly involved with Paul Johnson and his horse-owning set. In February she rode a fiery mare belonging to Reggie Trentham and broke her collar bone. Later, Paul Johnson invited her to go on a mysterious outing with him and Reggie

Trentham – it turned out to be a race meeting at Scowell Braddon where Paul's filly Christina was running. He had wanted Christine along for luck. Dan reprimanded her for going about with racy types.

At Phil and Grace's wedding, Jack was best man and Christine a bridesmaid.

John Tregorran quarrelled with Dr Cavendish, who had bought the Manor House from Squire Lawson-Hope and objected to John staging a 'Makemerry Fair' on his doorstep. John also quarrelled with Carol Grey, saying she was indiscreet to entertain Reggie Trentham until one o'clock in the morning. The next time John called, she refused to let him in. He told Tom that he was receiving so little co-operation for his 'Makemerry Fair' that he intended to hold it in Penny Hassett instead of Ambridge.

Christine passed her scooter test, and one of the Squire's former tenants, Joe Blower, bought a motor car. He then took Mrs P out for a ride in it, and made Walter jealous.

Peggy Archer (Thelma Rogers), Mrs P (Pauline Seville) and Jack Archer (Denis Folwell) discuss Jennifer's school report, 1954.

Doris spent much of the summer laying a crazy-paving path round her garden.

At the market garden, Carol found the work was getting on top of her, and Dr Cavendish came across her sobbing in the pump house. There was some slight relief when John Tregorran said he would not bother her again, but would divert his attention to a more responsive woman.

Phil was offered a directorship by Fairbrother, and arranged a dinner at Grey Gables with John Tregorran, Carol, and Reggie and Valerie Trentham as guests. During the evening the stables caught fire, and in trying to bring out Midnight, Grace was injured by a falling beam. She died in Phil's arms on the way to hospital.

After Grace's death, Paul Johnson and Chris drew closer together. He comforted her, and suggested joining her in a partnership at the stables. Doris moved into Coombe Farm with Phil for a short time.

At Brookfield, Dan had exceptionally good yields of wheat and barley, but his sugar beet suffered from drought.

On New Year's Eve, Walter threw a boisterous party at The Bull.

1956

This was the year of the great foot-and-mouth outbreak at Brookfield. On 17 January, two pigs were reported sick by Simon, and the vet was called. He suspected foot-and-mouth disease, and PC Bryden was ordered to stand guard on the gate to prevent anyone from entering or leaving. On 21 February, the outbreak was confirmed. All cloven-hoofed animals – cattle, sheep, and pigs – were slaughtered by humane killers. Len and Simon dug a pit to bury the carcasses. The cause of the disease was traced to some foreign liver which had accidentally been thrown into the swill bucket without being boiled.

Walter was pleased when Doughy Hood the baker returned to Ambridge, but disturbed to hear that Doughy was thinking of asking Mrs P to be his housekeeper. Doughy, however, had other problems on his mind. He believed John Tregorran was a rogue, but refused to say why for several weeks. It then emerged that a man called John Tregorran had swindled his friend out of a lot of money. Investigation proved that the villain was a Ron Tregorran. A penitent Doughy Hood offered to do a stall of decorative beads at John Tregorran's Whit Monday Fair.

Christine went into partnership at the stables with Paul Johnson's sister, Sally. When Paul proposed to her in June she accepted, and surprised her family by arriving home wearing an engagement ring.

Simon (Eddie Robinson) in the mangel clamp.

At Brookfield, Doris painted the kitchen scarlet and grey, and Dan thought about selling the farm and retiring. He asked Phil if his future plans included Brookfield, and Phil said 'no'. Jack said he was prepared to make a go of Brookfield for the sake of Anthony William Daniel. But Dan decided to cling on a bit longer.

Nelson Gabriel came home on leave and made unwelcome advances to Christine. She told him she was engaged but he persisted in being a nuisance. Paul heard about it and went out after Nelson's blood – Phil had to break up the fight.

Soon, to Walter's disappointment, Nelson said he had been recalled from leave and was being posted to one of the Mediterranean stations. Walter said he was thinking of giving up his farm – particularly as Fairbrother had confiscated ten acres of it. Phil planted potatoes on the ten acres, to clean the land ready for blackcurrants the following year.

Dan's bank manager advised him to get back into milk as soon as possible, and in October he bought seven cows and six new-calved heifers. Simon retired, and was replaced by Ned Larkin from Dorset. Dan's sheep were restocked with eighty Radnor-type ewes and two Downland rams.

Phil was given a cine camera for Christmas by Fairbrother, who said he wanted Phil to start a cine club in Ambridge. He gave Phil the camera early, so he could film Christine's wedding on 15 December. At the wedding, Christine wore a white lace dress with paper taffeta petticoats, and Doris wore an empire line dress of purple silk. Reggie Trentham was best man, and there was a reception at the Country Club.

A miserable Walter Gabriel finally decided to give up farming. He told Phil he would leave his farm next Lady Day.

1957

Ned Larkin's unmarried brother, Bob, followed him up from Dorset and annoyed Tom by making eyes at Pru Harris, the barmaid at The Bull. Not for long, however. Patrolling the woods one night with Phil, Tom struggled with a poacher and his gun went off. Bob Larkin was dead. Tom was arrested and charged with manslaughter. At Gloucester Assizes, several weeks later, he was found not guilty and made a triumphant return to Ambridge accompanied by the Borchester Silver Band.

In early March, Walter held a farm sale, and on Lady Day gave possession of his farm to Norman Wynford, who planned to keep a small dairy herd and fatten pigs for bacon. Walter bought a minibus and was granted a 'B' haulage and carrier's licence.

Phil became fascinated by cine photography, and made a film for the village cine club, with John Tregorran writing the script. Casting caused much jealousy in the village. In July he filmed the church fête, which was opened by Humphrey Littleton. He also filmed a very attractive girl with blonde, urchin-cut hair, wearing a yellow dress. A couple of weeks later he saw the girl again, demonstrating in a Borchester store. She told him her name was Jill Patterson, and she agreed to meet him at the Borchester Show.

At Brookfield, Dan received a telegram from his sister-in-law Laura in New Zealand to say his brother Frank was seriously ill. Next day he heard that Frank had died. Another telegram arrived at Brookfield when Dan and Doris were at the Three Counties Show, to say that Laura was in England and would arrive at Hollerton Junction that night. Phil went to meet her. Laura said she planned to stay in England for a while. Doris said she must regard Brookfield as her home.

June was dry and hot, with some of the highest temperatures for a hundred years. Walter began his carrier service in his minibus, and Mrs P bought him a spotlight for his birthday. His enthusiasm was

dashed, however, when teddy boys stole his bus from outside the
village hall. It was recovered with the seats slashed. Phil and John
Tregorran had them repaired for him.

Tom confessed to Doris that he was thinking of asking Pru Harris
to marry him, and Phil started seeing Jill Patterson frequently. She
told him she was an orphan. They met one day at New Street Station,
in Birmingham, and Phil asked her to marry him. She said she
needed time to think. A few weeks later they met for dinner at the
Station Hotel, Borchester. Phil remembered it was the second anniversary of Grace's death. They collected flowers together from the
garden of Coombe Farm and took them to the church.

At Brookfield, Dan discovered blight in his potato clamp, and
found he had lost twenty per cent of his crop, worth £160. He warned
his bank manager that he was going through a bad time.

Doris had her problems too, suffering from Laura's interference in
the way the house and farm were being run. Dan was about to tell
Laura to leave when she anticipated him by saying she had decided to
visit her friend Nellie Macdonald in Stourhampton. On the way she
was taken ill and rushed into Borchester General Hospital with a
mild form of heart trouble.

Jill finally agreed to marry Phil, and their wedding took place,
quietly, at Crudley church on 16 November. The Fairbrothers gave
them a second-hand car as a wedding present.

Peggy heard that Stourhampton Brewery were taking over The
Bull from Borchester Brewery.

1958

At Brookfield, Dan lost most of his oats when fire broke out in his
dutch barn. A casual labourer was blamed. Dan was financially hard-
hit, but refused an interest-free loan of £1,500 from Laura, who
offered him the money out of gratitude for his kindness, and because
he had gone to the trouble of finding her a cottage to rent in the
village.

In January, Lilian went skating on the village pond and fell
through the ice. She was rescued by Jack and Ned Larkin.

Walter Gabriel disappeared from Ambridge for a week, and on his
return admitted that he had had to clear Nelson's debts to get him
out of trouble. Walter himself was in trouble on Whit Monday, when
he blew a coaching horn at inappropriate moments during the
Ambridge-Penny Hassett cricket match. A few weeks later he puzzled Mrs P by giving her a silver locket and chain, 'in grateful thanks
for all her help and encouragement'.

Tom spent most of the spring and summer wondering whether or not to ask Pru Harris to marry him. He did ask her in the end, she accepted, and they were married on 26 September.

The big public controversy of the year was about a proposed arterial road – part of the Borchester bypass – which would cut through the Fairbrother Estate. Dan and John Tregorran organized a series of protest meetings, and the plan was finally abandoned.

Paul Johnson rode Monarch in the point-to-point at Heybury, but Doris refused to go and watch him. In the evening Dan discovered why: Doris had secretly been to the dentist and had all her teeth out.

Doris was spending every afternoon with Lettie Lawson-Hope, discussing old times. When Lettie died, she left Doris Glebe Cottage, with four acres of land, for her lifetime. Dan traced Boxer to a farm at Haddenwood, and borrowed him to partner Blossom for pulling the haywagon that carried Lettie's coffin to the church.

It was a wet summer, with heavy rain and severe thunderstorms in July. While Dan was helping at the church fête (opened by Squire Lawson-Hope), lightning struck an oak tree at Brookfield and killed six lambs.

John Tregorran took over running the village cine club from Phil, and also asked Doris if she would help to organize a folk music group in the village. Doris agreed, and suggested Jill as another possible organizer.

On 8 August, Jill gave birth to twins – and Dan was bewildered to find he had grandchildren called Kenton and Shula.

In the autumn there was a new apprentice at Brookfield, Jimmy Grange, who encountered a number of problems. First he borrowed Phil's cine camera and dropped it from his bedroom window, then he was almost accused of stealing the youth club funds, and finally a boy called Dusty Rhodes threw a brick through his guitar.

Carol Grey went on a sailing holiday with friends, and the village was alarmed to see a newspaper report that her boat had capsized off the coast of Denmark. But after several days she was reported to be safe and well.

Pru Forrest, though, was anything but well. After being X-rayed by a mobile chest unit she was sent to a sanatorium. The X-ray had showed a small patch on her lung, and she would be away from the village for two or three months.

At the end of the year, Dan decided to improve and reorganize Brookfield, and John Tregorran acted as Father Christmas at the Ambridge Christmas Fayre. Mrs Fairbrother resigned from the WI.

1959

As the year began, the village buzzed with the news that Fairbrother was selling his estate to an old friend of the Lawson-Hopes, Charles Grenville, who had just returned to England from Africa. As Fairbrother's farm manager, Phil met Grenville and decided he would be a dominating individual to work with.

Walter Gabriel was discovered ill in bed and feeling very neglected. Mrs P looked after him while John Tregorran took over his bus service. Walter later repaid Mrs P's kindness by rotovating her garden the evening after she had planted her seeds.

Stourhampton Brewery decided to sell The Bull, and gave Peggy and Jack the chance to buy it for £5,300. They were on the point of turning the offer down when Laura offered them an interest-free loan of £4,000, enabling them to go ahead with the purchase.

In March, Walter Gabriel had a biscuit tin of money stolen from his cottage, but the money was recovered by Tom and PC Bryden, who lay in wait at Arkwright Hall and caught a gypsy called Gregory Selden. It was, however, a trying year for Walter, who was becoming increasingly fond of Mrs P. In the summer Arthur Perkins came

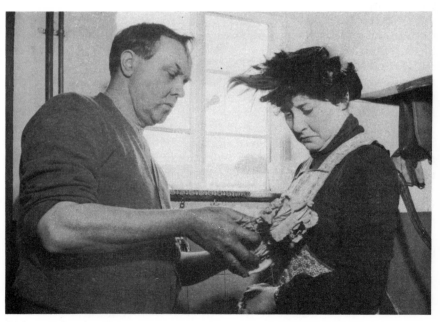

Walter Gabriel (Chris Gittins) and Mrs P (Pauline Seville) examine a cauliflower, 1954.

from London to work on a memorial window for Grace in the church, and Mrs P entertained him to several meals. Arthur soon proposed to Mrs P, who told him she could not consider remarriage at her age. A week or two later, however, she took him for a drive in her pony and trap and agreed to marry him. They left the village and set up home in London.

In June, Pru finally returned to Ambridge from the sanatorium, and Dan and Doris went to see Jimmy Grange and his skiffle group at a concert in Borchester. Doris thought the music terrible, but said young people ought to be encouraged to do their best.

Carol Grey was having problems with John Tregorran. She was late for a date one night, and found him half drunk in the Bear Hotel, Borchester. She took him home to Blossom Hill Cottage and was seen by Madame Garonne (Grenville's mysterious housekeeper) to leave at 1.30am. Then, in the summer Carol was asked by Grenville to step into the breach as hostess at a dinner party, after Madame Garonne had suddenly disappeared. She later dined alone with Grenville, and had to face the anger of a bitterly jealous John Tregorran.

Recovering from his disappointment over Mrs P, Walter decided to fatten and sell six pigs, and persuaded Ned Larkin to go into partnership with him.

In September, Dan was helping Ned to repair the roof of the implement shed when he fell and seriously injured himself on the binder. Phil and Tom freed him, and he was taken to hospital with a fractured leg. He returned home after several weeks, but refused to rest and had a bad fall in the dairy when his crutches slipped. Grenville told Phil to spend as much time as he needed running Brookfield while his father was ill.

On 18 September, Jill gave birth to a son, David Thomas.

Jimmy Grange was approached by an agent who wanted to promote him in show business. Jimmy, however, refused to be promoted without the rest of his skiffle group.

In the later autumn Carol Grey showed Grenville a copy of the *Borchester Echo* with headlines about Madame Garonne being a diamond smuggler.

Dr Maclaren sent Dan to hospital in Oxford with suspected pneumothorax, but it turned out to be a false alarm.

CHAPTER 3

Life on the Land

by Mollie Harris

Mollie Harris, who plays Martha Woodford, was brought up in Archers country and worked on the land herself in the early fifties. Here she recalls her experience as a seasonal worker and the world of The Archers in 1951, the year the programme started.

Winter '51

It was the noise of the threshing tackle rattling along the road past our cottage that woke me. It was Ben Todd and his gang and his threshing machine who, every year round about January or February time, came puffing in to the village to thresh out the corn ricks at several of the smaller farms in the area. Of course, the big farmers had already got combine harvesters but the not-so-well-off farmers were still using the binding machine to cut the corn at harvest time, with the farm hands stooking the sheaves of corn in the fields, where they stood for about three weeks before loading them up and carting them to the rickyards where the workers made great tidy ricks of them. Then, during the wintertime, when there was a bit of a lull on the land, the threshing of the corn ricks would be done.

Of course, it was only a matter of time before all the farmers, however small, would acquire a combine harvester and then the job of threshing would be a thing of the past. But while the threshers

Mollie Harris, potato-sorting in 1951.

came it meant that there would be some casual labour needed in the village for a couple of weeks or more.

Anyway, the previous year I had been too late to get a job threshing. It's a hard, dirty, dusty old job, but two shillings an hour is not to be sniffed at and for that money I was ready to put up with a bit of dust and dirt. So this time I leapt out of bed, determined to be pitching sheaves on Bill Banford's farm before nine o'clock. Middle Farm was always the threshing men's first port of call. I biked along to the rickyard where about eight fat, pregnant ricks stood, full of golden corn, rats and mice.

I went up to Ben Todd, the foreman. 'Any chance of a few days work?' I inquired.

He didn't look up from what he was doing, neither did he answer me, but just kept on working. I stood there defiant – at least I was the first woman on the scene, so he couldn't very well say I was too late. Two fit-looking pensioners were also waiting. Then the foreman slowly lit his pipe, carefully stamping out the lighted match afterwards. 'All right,' he said, gruffly, addressing all three of us.

'Be back here nine o'clock sharp. 'Course it'ull be ha'pas seven start after today.' He gave me an odd look; I found out later this was because I was not the usual woman he employed when he visited the village.

I tore off back home and looked out a pair of old trousers that I hadn't worn since the war, when I had driven a lorry for some time for a wholesale grocer. The trousers, though not very elegant, were a must. I dragged them on over my stockings, donned a couple of old jumpers and tied my hair up 'mammy' fashion, in a scarf. Looking at myself in the mirror, I remembered what my old granpa used to say about women who tied their hair up like that: 'They women's yeads looks fer all the world like a gret boiled puddin' tied up in an old puddin' cloth.' Still, at least the scarf would keep the dust and dirt away.

Suddenly I thought about dinner time and my husband coming home. Quickly I cut up some stewing beef, floured and seasoned it well, chucked in a couple of sliced onions and carrots and tipped it all into a casserole along with some bacon stock. A rice pudding and some jacket potatoes would cook at the same time as the slow-cooking stew, and all this would provide us with a reasonable dinner.

Then I was off down the road again, eager to start work.

'All right,' the foreman said. 'Up on that ladder and get the thatch off.'

God, that rick looked as high as the church tower. One of the other casual workers had gone up another ladder the other side and we reached the ridge together.

'Don't look down,' he said. 'Just strip off the thatch and chuck it down. Old Fred 'ull tidy it up.' The threshing machine had started up and was belching out thick black smoke that was blowing my way. It filled my eyes and throat, nearly choking me. As I coughed and spluttered, my workmate called, 'Fetch it up, it might be a tanner,' and we laughed as we scrambled back down the ladders.

A flurry of snow swept across the rickyard and the men banged their hands across their chests to warm them. Then Ben Todd came over and told us which job each of us had to do. Mine was to shin up to the top of the rick again and pitch the sheaves down on to the drum, where another man stood to receive them. With a sharp knife in his right hand and the sheaf of corn in his left, he quickly cut the binder twine immediately behind the knot, at the same time retaining the string in his left hand. This string was saved for a hundred-and-one uses on the farm. When he'd got about two dozen strings he would quickly loop them into a knot and toss them to the ground where somebody retrieved them. Mind you, at the same time that all this was going on he was feeding the sheaves to the ever-hungry drum and he had to work very fast because there were two of us pitching sheaves to him non-stop. Thump, thump, thump, the machine went as the sheaves passed through threshers and cutters and winnowers to come out the other end as lovely golden grain which poured into sacks that were carefully hooked on to the back of the drum. The men all worked as a team. One man took off a full sack and hooked another empty one on in its place, another wheeled the full ones away on an ancient sack truck and stacked the two hundredweight filled sacks into neat rows.

Another man made a rick of the straw which came out the back of the drum. This was barley straw and would most likely be used for bedding for the cattle. But when we got on to the wheat ricks, then the lovely long golden straw which came from them would be used for thatching cottages, ricks and barns. The chaff came out at another place; this had to be continuously shovelled away with a big flat wooden shovel. Later it was dumped in the farmyard where no doubt Mrs Banford's hens found great delight in scratching about in it.

I was so thankful when old Ben said that we could have ten minutes break. The farmer's wife brought out a great big jug of steaming hot cocoa and we stood about, drinking it. Then it was back to work again. Of course, it's quite easy pitching the sheaves down on to the drum and not too bad when you are working level with it, but when the rick has got down and you are two or three yards from the ground and you've got to pitch the sheaves *up*, that's when it becomes hard. I was thankful when it was twelve o'clock.

'All right,' the foreman said. 'Let's have you all back here at a quarter to one sharp.'

I pedalled off home, wondering what sort of reception I was going to get from my husband.

'What the hell do you think you are at, making a fool of yourself climbing about on a rick with a lot of men,' he said. All through the meal he was deadly quiet, then stormed out of the cottage mumbling about, 'A woman's place is in the home.'

Mind you, the way every bit of me ached I was almost willing to agree with him. Already I had got blisters on my hands and it seemed as if millions of barley hales – that's the little whiskers on the barley corn – had attached themselves to my vest and every other bit of clothing, making me itch like mad. Still, nothing could be done about that till the end of the day. I wondered how long I could stand the blisters and the itching and my poor stiff joints; then I thought of the two shillings an hour that I was going to get and set off for the afternoon's work quite cheerfully.

We had five minutes break halfway through the afternoon for a cup of tea, which again the farmer's wife brought out. This time she invited me into her warm kitchen.

'Have a bit of cake, Mollie,' she said. 'I got an extra pound of margarine yesterday from the shop and it's still eightpence a pound. I can't think why some people turn down their ration of marg. I can never seem to get enough with my hungry family to feed. They always come home starving and of course Bill eats like a horse. Still I suppose it's working outside in all weathers gives him such a good appetite.'

Before we had started work, one of the men had said to me, 'You be sure and tie some string tight round the bottoms of yer trouser legs, or some a they mice 'ull be taking a short cut up yer legs and we don't want that now do us.' Anyway we had just finished work on that first day and one of the casual workers, Jim Fitchett, was getting ready to go off home. He untied the string that had been round the bottoms of his trousers all day and walked across the rickyard to where his bike was. Just at that moment the farmer's little terrier rushed by, chasing a rat that had somehow been missed when we had got to the bottom of the rick. Quick as a flash, it shot up old Jim's trouser leg. I never saw anything like it in my life – talk about comic cuts. He danced about from one foot to the other, hollering and shouting and dancing about like a Red Indian doing a war dance. And all the time we others were laughing and shouting instructions as to what to do for the best. Then old Ben went up to him and shouted 'Take yer trousers off, man. 'Tis the only way to get rid of him.' And that's just what he did. Mind you, I didn't see that part of the operation. Modesty prevailed and I turned and looked the other way. After all, as my old gran used to say, 'A bit of fun's all right, but none of that.'

As soon as I got home I lit up my gas copper, first filling it with water. I'd have a bath as soon as the water was hot enough. I went outside and lifted our tin bath from its hook on the outside wall at the back of the cottage and set it down in the kitchen next to the gas copper. Oh, such luxury, sitting in that bath at half-past four in the afternoon, the hot soapy water seeming to draw all the aches from my body. A clean vest was most important and before I washed the one I had been wearing all day, I had to sit and pick out the barley hales. They would never have come out with just washing.

So the work went, day after day, until all the local farms had been visited by the threshers.

But before the threshing gang left the village to go to the next hamlet a few miles away, old Ben Todd, a man of few words, did come up and thank me. Then he asked if I would like to go with him and help out, but it meant a ride of six miles there and back to the next job, and that along with the work and my housework would be stretching it a bit, so I declined his offer. Anyway he told Mr Banford that I was the best woman worker he had ever employed.

Early spring '51

But that bout of threshing started something for me, because about a week or so after we had finished, one of the foremen from a big farm about a couple of miles away called to see if I would help with the potato sorting. It would mean working outside in a field all day, he said. Well, I didn't mind that and started the next morning. The potatoes were stored in a great big long clamp along-side the edge of the field, like a great long roof it looked. Goodness knows how many hundreds of tons it held.

Two of the workmen were busy taking off layers of soil from the clamp. You see, in the autumn when the potatoes had been harvested, they were first heaped up on the ground, the layers of yelmed straw were laid all over them and then a foot or more of earth on the top. This was to keep the crop dry and free from frost.

When the men had uncovered what they thought we might do in the morning, we started to sort the spuds. They daren't expose too many at a time, because the weather was cold and potatoes soon catch the frost. At the front of the clamp there was a machine called a potato riddler, powered by a small Lister engine. One of the men shovelled the spuds into the machine with an eight- or ten-pronged fork which had small nobbles on the ends of the prongs so as not to jab the spuds. They spun round in a sort of cage affair that knocked off most of the mud and dirt – at the same time the very small 'pig' potatoes dropped through the mesh wire on to the floor. The rest of them travelled up a slatted conveyor belt to where two of us stood, one on either side. It was our job to pick off any rotten, green or very misshapen ones and drop them into a sack which hung by our sides. (These again would be sold as 'pig' potatoes.) The good ones – 'Ware' they were called – travelled on to the end to drop into waiting sacks that were hooked on to the end of the belt. Here a man took full sacks off, hung back empty ones, weighed them to one hundred-weight and sewed up the tops with a bagging needle and bagtie string, then stacked them in neat one-ton rows. As we used the spuds up from the clamp, we stopped about every hour to push the machine up closer to it. Every afternoon before we left work, a wholesaler's

lorry would come and pick up all the sacks of potatoes that we had
sorted.

All went well for a couple of days, then the farmer wanted one of
the men to go drilling corn and asked if I could get another woman
from the village to come along. That was easy; there were several I
knew that would only be too glad to come. Our pay was two and
sixpence an hour, and we were allowed to take home a good boiling
of spuds each evening. In fact we always found something to take
home. We used to fill up our bicycle baskets with potatoes and kin-
dling wood, and for a few days one of the farm workers was laying
a hedge nearby and he gave us lovely chunky pieces of blackthorn
wood. Of course, that burns like coal so we never said no to it.

By the end of the first week we had an all-woman team. The cold
dry winds of March kept the rest of the farm workers busy drilling
corn and harrowing. We only had half an hour for dinner so that the
women would be home that much earlier in the afternoon, before
the children came home from school. We used to sit on sacks of
spuds to have our sandwiches and flasks at twelve o'clock. We all
began to look very weatherbeaten and healthy and quite enjoyed
ourselves singing and laughing all day long. As sweet rationing was
still on, each day one of us would bring a few sweets in turn. It was
pretty dry work I can tell you with the dust coming off the spuds.

I remember one afternoon we were all cycling home and we kept
meeting posh limousines coming up the road, Humbers, Rolls and
Rovers. Then we realized that it was Gold Cup day at Cheltenham
and these were the wealthy rich cruising home. I remember too the
hedgerows were just beginning to burst out with the young, green
hawthorn leaves, that lovely delicate green that only lasts a week or
two. Now every spring when I first see them coming out and eat
some (bread and cheese we called it as youngsters), I'm reminded of
those hard-working, happy days we spent 'tater-sorting.

No sooner had the sorting finished when the farmer asked two of
us to go potato planting. We arrived at the field on a fine spring
morning. A small grey Ferguson tractor was already ticking over.
Over the back of this was fixed a potato hopper, a big, funnel-like
contraption that held three or four hundredweight of seed potatoes
at a time. Under the hopper was a sort of three-furrow boulting-out
plough; it's a plough with two mould boards which make deep chan-
nels to plant the spuds in.

We had to perch ourselves on two metal seats facing each other.
As soon as the tractor started moving down the field the potatoes
began to drop on to a small ledge in front of us. There was a little
automatic bell fixed on the machine and every time it rang you

dropped a seed potato down a little chute in front of you. Ping, ping, ping, ping, the bell went as we planted acres of spuds during the next ten days.

The fields that we were working in were away from the road and we saw flowers and birds and animals that we wouldn't otherwise have seen – banks of primroses and violets and cowslips in bud, brown trout in the river that edged one of the fields and one day the tractor driver showed us a badger's set.

By the end of the planting we were helping Fred the driver fill up the hopper with seed spuds, tipping one hundredweight sacks into the hopper quite easily. Mind you, we both breathed a sigh of relief when the manager came to say that he wouldn't be needing us again for several weeks. After all, there was the spring cleaning to do, blankets to wash and all manner of things to see to both in the house and flower garden.

Late spring

We had hardly got the spring cleaning done before two of us were asked to go singling sugar beet and swedes. That was one of the worst jobs I think I've ever had to do on a farm. The sun bore down on the dusty fields as, heads down, we chopped away at the everlasting rows of plants with our hoes. One of the days was brightened a bit when an old shepherd joined us. He told us all sorts of earthy stories. It was he who introduced us to 'sheeps dags' – 'fer yer kidley beans,' he told us. 'You see,' he said, 'when you dags um, thas what you calls it when you 'as to cut them lumps of wool and muck awf thur backsides, affore shearin' time. Well, you wants to get 'old a some a they dags if you can, lay um in her kidley bean trench and you'll 'ave beans a yard long.'

Well, just a few days after we had finished the hoeing, up came the foreman to ask me to go and help the shepherd dag the sheep! I had to catch the ones with dirty backsides and hold them while the shepherd cut round their backpart with a pair of handclippers – a filthy old job, but quite rewarding. I was presented with a huge sack of daggings at the end of the day that I proudly carried home on my bike. He was right about their being good for kidney beans; we had a most bountiful crop that year.

Summer

After the dagging I had quite a long break. I was glad to; there were
WI outings to go on and the cricket teas to help with on Saturday
afternoons, school holidays and the soft fruit to be bottled and made
into jam. Sugar was sevenpence halfpenny for two pounds and I
bought quite a lot during the summer months. Our few hens were
laying well so I bought a tin of water glass. With this costing one and
fourpence halfpenny a tin, you could 'preserve' or put down lots of
eggs. I first mixed the water glass with water, then tipped it into an
old bucket or earthenware jar, and as the hens laid the eggs I just
carefully set them in the liquid. Then, when the wintertime came
and the hens were not laying so well, all I had to do was dip my hand
in and take them out of the bucket. Mind you, I used them for
cooking mostly, in cakes and puddings.

It was lovely weather during June and July, and our garden was a
picture, full up with every flower imaginable; it's an old-fashioned
cottage garden and there's always something blooming in there any
time of the year. When the cricket team played away, we mums and
children used to hie ourselves down to the riverside. We would each
take plenty of food, one would bring the kettle and another a teapot.
I used to take an old primus stove and we would boil up the water
for the tea on it. Oh, they were super days. The children played –
and fought – and we grown-ups just sat and chatted and enjoyed the
surroundings. We stayed there till quite late in the evenings, then
when all the food was gone and the children tired, we made our way
home. Lovely, unforgettable summer days.

About the second or third week in July the foreman came to ask if
I would help with the corn harvest, on the back of a brand new
combine. The 'cut' was quite a narrow one, at least to what we were
to see during the next few years. Nevertheless, the first day had me
jumping about on the back, I can tell you. It was my job to hook the
sacks on to the back to collect the corn in – just the same method as
on the back of the threshing drum. While the right-hand sack was
filling I had quickly to take the full one off from the left-hand side.
Then I had to drag it a few feet across the steel platform and tie the
neck very securely with string. These sacks weighed two hundredweight so they took a bit of manoeuvring. Then I had to let it down
a chute on to the field. By the time I had done this *and* fixed an
empty sack on the left side, the other sack was brim full.

I remember the second day at this job the driver disturbed a hor-
nets' nest. It was quite frightening really, those great big buzzing
insects following us up and down in that field for quite a while. We

thought that we would never get rid of them. I suppose really they were searching for their nest that we had wrecked.

The combine, this type anyhow, was one of the first of its kind in the area and most days, if we were working in a field next to the roadway, we had quite a number of spectators. The local farmers came along too.

Another day during harvest I had a change and worked on the straw baler. I had to stand on a wooden sledge that was fixed to the back of the baler, and there was nothing at all to catch hold of. As the baler thumped the tight bales out I had to catch them and slide them on to this wooden sledge, stacking them three across and three high. There was a slit cut halfway down the back of the sledge. When I'd got nine bales on there, I had to pick up a seven foot long iron bar (which was lying on the sledge) and thrust it into the slot and at the same time push my body against the bales. If you had stacked them right they would simply slide off the sledge and on to the field still stacked. Mind you, if the ground was a bit muddy you could end up on the end of the iron bar, which happened to me a couple of times, just like some folk end up on the end of punt poles. As time went on you could stack more than nine bales on your sledge, but nine was certainly enough to start with.

Midway through August on this particular farm saw the corn harvest well under way. And I wouldn't be needed again for a while. But the foreman went on, 'Come the end of September, beginning of October, I shall need about twenty women for potato picking. There will be getting on for three weeks work. If you like,' he said, 'you can get a gang together ready. Transport would be provided.'

Of course the local women were delighted to hear this news; there wasn't much other work about for housewives in 1951. But those few weeks off between harvest and the potato picking gave me the chance to get on with the pickling, bottling and chutney making. I sat outside in the garden and did the shallots (sharlots one of my old country friends calls them), crying as they always make me, no matter what folks say about peeling them under water, or holding a tablespoon in your mouth as you do them. I made pounds of green tomato chutney and piccalilli. I don't think there is a better picture come autumn time than the larder shelves filled with bottles of fruit and vegetables and jams and jelly.

Autumn

Well, come September I got my 'gang' together. We looked a motley
crowd on that first day as we stood waiting for the tractor and trailer
to pick us up. Some of us had trousers on – some of which belonged
to husbands. Long skirts, short skirts, sons' or husbands' welling-
tons, old macs and jackets and a bright array of head scarves. Young
children under school age came along with their mothers. We were
all raring to go and the chatter from twenty excited women sounded
like dozens of chickens in a deep litter house.

Not only did we go potato picking for the big farm, but three
other smaller farmers employed us for a few days as well. At the big
farm we did not start work until the middle of October – the first
week was fine and dry and we got on very well. Then it was 'stop'
and 'go', we would have two days rain and then three or four dry
ones. The work, of course, is much harder when it's muddy and it
proved too much for some of us, especially the ones with young
children, and our gang diminished by about a third. Some days we
had just settled down to a good pace, with the old spinner chucking
the spuds out for us to pick up, when the heavens would open and
down the rain would come. When it looked like settling in for the
day there was nothing for it but to pack up and go home on the back
of an open trailer, looking a sorry sight too. The foreman was a bit
of a slave-driver, he was eager to get the spud crop in the clamps
before the weather got worse. I thought he was pushing us a bit too
hard and suggested to the gang (by now I was considered to be
official ganger) that I might try to get us a bit more money. We were
still only getting half a crown an hour. At the beginning of the third
week I tackled him – another tuppence an hour we wanted for the
pace that we were working. He went very red in the face and said,
'Ah, what about all those pounds of spuds they take home in their
dinner bags each night?'

'Pickers' perks,' I said.

'I'll let you know tomorrow first thing,' he replied. And that was
it, we got our rise and the women were jubilant.

My last job on the farm that year was pulling and cleaning swedes
and mangolds and helping to lift the sugar beet, those that we had
carefully singled earlier in the year. I was quite pleased with my
earnings and promptly bought a good second-hand carpet at a furniture sale. It completely covered our sitting-room floor; up till then
the stone slabs had been covered with coconut matting.

It was amazing how quickly the scene on the land was changing.
The back end of that year found old Ben retired from his traction

engine and threshing machine. By the following year most of the farmers had got at least one tractor – they could set this up, and providing they could get hold of a threshing drum, they could thresh their own corn, if they wanted barley for fattening the pigs or some-one needed straw for thatching. Those who couldn't afford a com-bine could pay a contractor to come and do it or borrow one from a neighbour. The big waggon-loads of sheaves of corn grew less, so did the stooks in the harvest fields, and the lovely shire horses that had loyally pulled those loads for years went off to the knacker's yard.

But for me it was the beginning of a new era. During the next nine or ten years I learned to do every job there was to do on a farm, and enjoyed doing it. Some of the villagers who saw me coming home after a day's work, maybe covered up to my knees in mud, used to say, 'You must want your head seeing to, working in those conditions.' But I think the reason I enjoyed it so was my great love of the land and the countryside, and the fact that my forebears had been yeomen farmers in Gloucestershire for years.

The Sixties

CHAPTER 4

The Archers' Story II

by Jock Gallagher

At the beginning of a new decade and with the programme moving into its own tenth year, The Archers received an accolade accorded few soap-operas, a full-blown critical assessment on the BBC's Third Programme. The attention of such a highbrow programme as *The Critics* might not have meant much to the average Archers listener, but to the programme's professionals, it was important in that it showed that their work was being taken seriously, that it had some literary merit and that they were making a contribution to the broadcasting arts. Its value in this historical perspective is that the discussion between three respected critics – Lionel Hale, Ivor Brown and David Sylvester – offers a rare, objective view of The Archers' impact and achievements in those first nine years.

Lionel Hale opened the discussion with an admission that he had not listened to the programme for one or two years, but on returning to it, he had felt a welcome sense of familiarity. He commented too on the authenticity of its presentation of country and community life, but then came to what he considered to be the real question.

The Archers is immensely popular with a mass of people who have little contact with the country, as well as with country-dwellers. The Ambridge family has enlarged itself to include a family of listeners wherever the BBC is heard, and they feel intensely that they, themselves, are part of something real. This can't have been done just on a homely mixture of rustics, some of them a little theatrical, and little boy-and-girl romances, or domestic tiffs, and it surely can't have been because it often has a sort of propaganda information purpose. I feel that somehow it appeals to a lot of people, who may well have lost in their own lives, the fullness of a family. Perhaps this leans a bit seriously on it, but if this isn't so, how do you account for the devoted host of listeners to The Archers, even if is, purely as radio, well and solidly done? How do you account for it?

That is, of course, the question always being asked of The Archers. There does not appear, even after thirty years, to be a definitive answer, but Ivor Brown had a go:

I think the interesting thing about these serials on the BBC is they are doing, in a way, what some of the second-rank Victorian novelists did, and that is giving you a picture of society, of a family, which you do identify yourself with and want to learn about. I am thinking of the series like the Trollope Barchester novels, the Trollope political novels, and a Victorian writer I'm very fond of, Charlotte Young, who took you into a big family and gave you various family relationships and you can read them very slowly; well the modern public hasn't got so much time for reading and they sit and listen to it happening on the wireless. . . . It seems to me that there are three things that most of the listeners want from The Archers. One is to have a vicarious family, which is extremely important. Another is going back to the country; and the one that summarizes both of them is a sense of security. You know that if you switch on at a quarter-to-seven you've got that family atmosphere for at least a quarter-of-an-hour . . . I mean, it is part of the social structure of the life of this country by now, isn't it?

Having heard the other two struggle for answers, David Sylvester simply gave up.

I don't know anything about this programme, except that I'm one of the devoted hosts of listeners, although I'm not quite. I'm a devoted listener for several months at a time. I never miss an omnibus edition, and often hear it in the evenings as well at 6.45 and then after a few months I get exasperated, get tremendously indifferent towards The Archers, forget about them for several months. Then I tune in again, possibly by chance or through boredom, and I find myself a devoted listener again for several months. But I really don't know why I do it.

That can be taken as fairly substantial evidence that, however it was managing it, The Archers was getting across to even the most discriminating listener. But around this time, a series of behind-the-scenes problems was beginning to catch up with the programme-makers, making it more and more difficult for the writers to go on getting their message across. Like any group of people, those involved with The Archers had, over the years, suffered their fair share of colds, 'flu and other assorted ailments, and usually the writers had been able to cope by making minor adjustments to the scripts to allow the particular actor or actress either to have a cold in the programme, or to be laid up in bed if it was a bit more serious. In 1959, however, Harry Oakes became quite ill and had to go into hospital for a prolonged period. At first it was felt that the answer was for Dan, too, to go into hospital and this was duly written into the script. Then it was realized that Harry was going to be out of action for much longer than Dan's absence from the programme would be accepted, without concern, from the listeners. It was a dilemma which the production team were to face on several subsequent occasions, but this was the first and therefore most agonizing. Discussions were protracted. Because it had not been the practice before, it was too late to follow the theatrical example of having stand-ins for the main characters without its somehow underlining the worry about Harry Oakes's health. Inevitably, the debate was taken one step further: what if one of the leading artistes died? Some people thought the part should be re-cast, others thought the character should also die. With memories of Grace much in their minds, it was finally agreed that it would be too harrowing for the audience if the artiste and character both died and therefore that the only solution was in fact to find stand-ins. In February, 1960, Monte Crick was auditioned and offered a contract to shadow Dan Archer. When Harry Oakes died later in the following year, Monte Crick took over the part permanently and the listeners seemed none the wiser.

Harry's illness had also raised for the first time questions about the long-term future of the programme. It had originally been conceived as a three-month venture and, partly through nervousness as to what the answer might be, and partly because of the assembly-line nature of the daily production, no one seemed to have considered looking years ahead. Even producer Tony Shryane was still on a temporary contract. Now, although it was settled for the foreseeable future, one or two people began to ask who would become the central characters once Dan and Doris became too old. Brookfield Farm without Dan and Doris was clearly too much for most people to consider and, as a consequence, no firm conclusion was reached. The line between fiction and reality, already blurred for so many of the programme's listeners, seemed none too clear to the professionals and it would appear that no one wanted to accept any kind of responsibility for ending the days of Britain's best-loved couple. It would have to be left to another generation of writers to make that decision. What did happen, however, was an acknowledgement that there could be a long and happy future for the programme: a far-sighted piece of family-planning was initiated which, with appropriate marriages and births, would establish an Archer dynasty from which later writers could find the new central characters when they were needed. It was a masterly compromise.

Concurrent with that debate was another that very clearly shows the way Britain's social climate was changing. A couple of years earlier, when the writers suggested that the marriage of Christine and Paul Johnson was somewhat shaky, they had been cautioned not to make any mention of divorce. Now, when they raised the subject again, it still had to be referred upwards, but this time it was agreed to (although as it happened, the pair never were divorced). When it was eventually broached on the air – after Paul had been caught seeing an old girlfriend – there was only one complaint, albeit a strong one: 'My wife and I have listened to The Archers for many, many years and we both feel strongly about this scandal with Paul Johnstone and Marie Ann. Please end it and without a divorce. Please. They are supposed to be working-class folk, well, they do not have divorces. One scene last week almost sounded like *Lady Chatterley's Lover*. Country folk are clean and good-living, not like the so called upper town class.'

Among the many souvenirs that Tony Shryane has collected in his twenty-eight years as producer, is one that represents another rare tribute to soap-opera, a framed copy of a leader from *The Times*. It was published to mark the programme's tenth anniversary and one can, perhaps, detect in the generous tribute the hand of *The Times* editor Sir William Haley, who had been the BBC's Director-General in 1951, when The Archers was launched. Its origination was recalled in the leader's simple headline, 'A farming *Dick Barton*'.

> The formula for The Archers – a farming family serial composed of ninety per cent entertainment and ten per cent information – does not, on paper, seem to have the promise of a great national success. Yet rarely can a long-running success have more naturally and more inevitably asserted itself . . . What is the secret of it all, and is there a moral?
>
> . . . The programme is always authentic. It therefore rings true

to both countryman and townsman. It keeps farmers informed of agricultural developments. A feeling is thus given that The Archers is not just a tale that is told but something that is happening here and now . . . Whether it is because of wide-spread loneliness, whether it is the satisfaction of becoming absorbed in a continuing simple human drama as an escape from a world in which so much is disjointed, complicated and inhuman, whether it is that the call of the land is heard by all, The Archers formula has never had to be varied. The clever and the smart may be superior about it, but it deals with enduring things. And they do endure.

And having lasted ten years was a feat of endurance by the programme itself, or more accurately by the small team that had remained unchanged throughout. For Godfrey Basely, Tony Shryane, Ted Mason and Geoff Webb, the everyday story of country-folk had in fact been an almost everyday and every waking-hour, all-consuming experience. The relentless hunger for new stories, new situations, new characters had meant little spare time for the four men. Under such circumstances, ten years is a very long time. Not surprisingly, the strain began to tell. It was not very much to begin with – the odd comment when somebody had not told somebody else what they were up to; a bit of back-biting when a script was a day or two late in arriving; some general complaining about the restrictions caused by a limited budget. They were all natural irritations which often arise in a small group working very closely together, but when they started to show in the quality of the script and production, they could be blown up out of proportion:

Yesterday, with one of the main news stories of the day that not a single part of the United Kingdom had any ice or snow during the previous week (based, you remember, on an RAC report), we go out on a rickety limb and talk about the arctic conditions at Ambridge, where it is so cold that farming can hardly continue and where pipes in Carol's roof are frozen solid – which takes a lot of doing – despite the fact that an old oak beam a few yards away from them is smouldering. I wonder how many degrees of frost this would call for! We should, I think, have spotted this at this end, had we the scripts in time.

This note is only sent in a spirit of helpfulness in relation to the future. No scalps are required or wanted, but do look into it and see if what appeared a very stupid incident was my fault, the writer's fault or the producer's fault, or who you will.

The jollifications surrounding the anniversary must have seemed a

long way back at that stage. But sadly, the problems caused by the
pressures were really just beginning. Geoff Webb's health began to
deteriorate and this threw an even greater burden on Ted Mason.
Reluctantly, it was accepted that it was no longer possible to survive
on the old team and another writer must be brought in. But that was
not as easy as one might think. Writing for radio drama was highly
specialized and writing for a long-running serial was even more so,
because of the need to be able to assimilate all the idiosyncrasies of
dozens of characters and to absorb all the incidents that had already
taken place. Eventually, the Birmingham playwright David Turner
was recruited, but only on a temporary basis. With the success of his
Semi-Detached in the West End, the theatre was very much his first
love and he did not want to give it up. So for a while, Ted wrote
most of the scripts, Geoff wrote when he could, and David took on
the rest.

This was clearly not the happiest of times for The Archers and
insecurity is writ large in most of the memos and letters. Sometimes
cracks in the teamwork threatened to become chasms, niggles to
become major issues. Even long-standing personal friendships were
being stretched close to breaking-point. Then, suddenly, the gloom
was lifted. Tony Shryane was awarded the MBE in the Queen's
Birthday Honours and everyone felt entitled to share the warm glow
of satisfaction that the efforts of the ten long years had not gone
unnoticed. While the team was fully justified in sharing the glory, it
is also true that Tony Shryane's personal contribution had been
unique. Although his first couple of months had been under Godfrey
Baseley's supervision, Tony had produced every single one of the
2,700-plus episodes. One does not have to know what producing a
programme entails to recognize that as a remarkable achievement.

In The Archers, the producer is the fulcrum and pivoting on him
are the script-writers and editor, the technicians and the actors and
actresses. He is also the businessman, controlling the use of resources
and the budget. It is not a job for the faint-hearted. He must be able
to interpret the aspirations of the writers and the intent of the editor.
He has to explain his requirements to the technicians. He has to
direct the cast. And he has to do it all within a rigidly-controlled
time-scale and for an even more rigidly-controlled amount of
money. All that, though, could be as child's-play without another
key factor – the creative temperament. Writers and actors are not
exactly noted for their equanimity, nor are they the most selfless of
individuals. Within The Archers, it is quite clear that a number of
highly-emotional storms often endangered the programme. But

Tony Shryane at an editing session with Valerie Hodgetts, the programme's production assistant, who later became his wife.

Tony Shryane rode them all and always managed to restore calm where it mattered most, in the studio.

When he first took on The Archers, as has already been noted, the programme too was on trial and Tony was therefore not allowed to devote all his time to it. This meant he had to organize things very tightly, and from that developed a style that stayed with him throughout his career. When The Archers proved successful, he could easily have persuaded his boss that a five-days-a-week programme *was* a full-time job. He did not bother and instead turned his fertile mind into devising and producing other successful programmes: *Guilty Party* (a crime quiz featuring F. R. Buckley, John Arlott and Fabian of the Yard) which ran from 1953 to 1956; *My Word* (in which Frank Muir and Denis Norden first appeared as performers) in 1956; and *My Music* in 1965. All three programmes he devised with Ted Mason and, of course, both *My Word* and *My Music* are still running very successfully, with Tony still very much involved, despite his formal retirement.

Throughout the rest of 1961 and into the next year, Geoff Webb's health continued to be delicate and his contributions to the programme became spasmodic. It was a great pity, because Geoff was a remarkable character. On one occasion there was a mix-up in the writing schedules, which left Ted Mason thinking Geoff was responsible for a particular fortnight's script and Geoff thinking Ted was responsible. Unaware of the confusion, the producer's patience finally ran out on a Friday afternoon, when he still had not received the scripts for the following Monday's production in the studio. He rang Ted Mason. 'Not my turn, old boy,' said Ted. He rang Geoff, who started to say the reverse was the case, when Tony Shryane anxiously interrupted. Without further ado, Geoff jumped in his car, drove to the Birmingham office and immediately set to writing the ten scripts. It took him two days, working almost non-stop, but the scripts were ready for the cast when they arrived and the quality of the writing was every bit as good as it had always been. The only ill-effect on Geoff was a rash he developed from an old blanket he had found and used to keep himself warm as he dozed off between typing-sessions. Even when Geoff finally had to go into hospital, he still went on writing occasional scripts. He returned home in June 1962 and seemed to be on the mend. Then one day he was out in his car, was involved in an accident and died from his injuries. This was the first of several deaths that were to hit the team, and it came as a terrible shock.

When the hurt finally subsided a little, the remaining members reluctantly had to face the problem of finding a replacement writer. At a meeting to discuss the matter, the Head of Light Programme said he thought it essential that the new writer had a rural background and he suggested that four to six writers be asked to do a sample five episodes each, then a shortlist of two be asked to ghost the programme for a while before the final choice. It was a fairly lengthy procedure and it was some months before the winner was announced – John Keir Cross, a Scotsman, then living in the West Country. John was a novelist who had also written previous successful radio programmes, but more importantly perhaps, he and Ted Mason were friends, who had once collaborated in writing a thriller for Radio Luxembourg. At John's first script-conference, he was told: 'What we need is more humour, more sex, more drama . . . and a strong carry-over from the Friday to the Monday episode!' Lest Lord Reith should start to turn in his grave, it should be stressed that what was then being advocated was not the kind of sex – full frontal and so on – that is commonplace today, but more of a healthy rural awareness of the birds and the bees and the effects of the sap rising in the spring-time. Even so, the very use of the word showed how much Britain's attitudes had changed from the mid-fifties to the early sixties. No doubt the wireless people put such changes down to the steady growth of television.

Both the BBC and commercial channel were, of course, very firmly established by now. Indeed, the Pilkington Committee on Broadcasting had just reported to the government with proposals that included the setting up of a third channel – BBC2. Radio had already lost a lot of listeners to such popular television programmes as *Dr Finlay's Casebook, Z Cars*, and the fledgling *Coronation Street*. Although Sir Harry Pilkington himself stressed that 'it would be a mistake to underestimate the importance of sound radio', the nervousness of all those involved with The Archers served to keep them very much on their toes. Storylines were made more dramatic – Phil Archer had some of his cattle rustled and Jack Woolley, the rough diamond, arrived from Birmingham to disrupt the rural calm of Ambridge – and Tony Shryane was at even greater pains with his production, so successfully that it brought this note from his boss; 'I have noticed some very good effects in The Archers lately – which does not mean, by implication, that I have not heard them in the past! – and this is just to say thank you very much for all the ever fresh enthusiasm which you put into the show year after year. I thought that the tiny noise of Walter Gabriel's chair being pushed back as he got up from Dan Archer's table on Sunday was first-rate radio.'

First-rate radio or not, it did not stop the slow drift to television, nor did it stop a growing number of complaints, 'on the subject of smoking, alcohol and lavatory humour'. With something approaching despair, the writers decided again to turn to death, only this time it would be a double tragedy involving John Tregorran's wife Janet and Charles Grenville. But then they had second thoughts: 'Godfrey Baseley reported (to a script-conference) that after some disagreement, he and the writers had finally decided on the following action . . . Charles and Janet will be involved in a car accident in which Janet will be killed instantly. Charles will not be killed after all, but will sustain severe injuries which will necessitate him being in hospital for some time.' This time there was no discussion in which scruples and consciences could be paraded, another sign of the changing times.

Although it did not have the same stunning effect of the Grace Archer incident, the death had a strong impact on many listeners:

'You've done it again. First it was Grace Archer and now Janet Tregorran. There's only one word for it – murder.'

'Tony Shryane, I hate you, I hate you, oh I hate you! I didn't

mind when Grace bought it. Her voice always did drive me up
the wall, but that nice nurse. It's a damn rotten shame getting rid
of her like that . . .'

'May I quote my reactions to last evening's episode of The
Archers. For quite a while I have been very disinterested and felt
there was too much propaganda and got quite bored at times. I
wasn't listening too deeply last evening, but by jove the shock of
realizing what had happened made me sit bolt upright, and now I
can't wait for the programme to continue. Our interest is now
restored in our very much loved Archer family . . .'

The reaction expressed in that last letter was, of course, exactly what
the writers were after. The death showed that there was still plenty
of life left in the daily serial.

But all the ups and downs (and it has to be said that there were
rather more downs that ups) had had a bad effect on the cast, and
when there was talk of moving the Sunday omnibus edition from the
Light Programme to the Home Service, the insecurity spilled out
into the open. The actors and actresses did not understand the move,
which was part of a reorganization of radio, and they saw it as a
precursor to the programme being taken off altogether. In their
anxiety that that should not happen, they said they wanted to be
more closely involved in the programme's production. They asked
for a meeting 'to represent the feelings of at least half a dozen of the
cast; that they should in fact put forward suggestions, based on their
own experiences and contacts outside, for the writers to use, and also
that they should be informed ahead of the story-line development,'
From Godfrey and the writers, the response was cool: 'On our side
of the fence, we would certainly not dream of doing either thing, as
we feel we are quite capable of providing the right kind of material
for the programme, and that they, as actors, should be quite capable
of interpreting what is written down on paper for them. Tony is
always in the picture so far as future developments are concerned,
and I know he can and does direct the cast very successfully through
any scenes that have a direct bearing on the future.' No more was
heard of the matter. But just in case the writers felt anything close to
smugness at having simply shrugged off that threat, they themselves
got a rap on the knuckles. 'The dialogue is in the wrong idiom for
the young people of today,' they were told. 'If you must use slang,
kindly see that it is at least contemporary slang.' It is surprising the
number of times the writers stood such curt directives and it says
much for their professionalism that they never let the schoolmasterly
language bother them. They realized that under the relentless pres-

sure of writing a daily serial, they needed other people to keep a
critical eye on the scripts and their instinctive responses were clearly
tempered by gratitude.

The weekend of the omnibus edition's move to the Home Service,
Frank Gillard, Director of Sound Broadcasting, tried to put it in
perspective in an article in *Radio Times*: 'Developments of major
importance are impending in Sound Broadcasting. This weekend the
BBC is introducing the first step in the most ambitious programme
of expansion to be undertaken since domestic radio began in Britain
forty-two years ago.' This, he said, included an increase of nearly an
extra one hundred hours of broadcasting a week, mainly on the
Third and Light Programmes. He went on:

> Fifteen hours or so of the Light Programme's 20½ hour broad-
> casting day will be of gay and cheerful music, suited to the general
> character of the Programme. About 4½ hours of this music will
> come from gramophone records. The BBC's quota of needle-time
> allows only this relatively small ration of records for the Light
> Programme, and this fact will perhaps reassure those who fear that
> the Light is going all-pop. Current popular numbers will of course
> be much heard, but they will not predominate.
>
> Alongside this copious output of musical entertainment the
> Light Programme will retain its popular radio plays and serials, its
> comedy shows, *Woman's Hour*, *Radio Newsreel* and other estab-
> lished features. But the Home Service, which will be transferring
> some of its daytime music to the Third Network, will be taking
> over a few regular items from the Light, ranging from *Down Your
> Way* and *Chapel in the Valley* to the Sunday morning *Archers'
> Omnibus* and, from next week, *Listen with Mother*. We hope listen-
> ers will soon find their way about in this minor reshuffle.

To help those Archer listeners who could not find their own way
to the Home, the people unlucky enough to be manning the telephones on the Sunday morning were given a special briefing and a
short message for callers: 'The BBC's output in radio is being
extended and this has resulted in a number of changes, all of which
are shown in the *Radio Times*. The Archers' omnibus will, from now
on, be on the Home Service instead of the Light Programme, but at
the same time. All you have to do is switch to the Home Service and
you will get it.' But more than half the supposedly-devoted listeners
did not make the switch. Instead of taking a vicarious walk in the
fresh, clean air of Ambridge, something like two million people
simply stayed indoors and listened to the 'gay and cheerful music' on

On the left, Bill Payne (Ned Larkin), and right: Bob Arnold (Tom Forrest), being served in The Bull by Dennis Folwell (Jack) and Thelma Rogers (Peggy)

the Light Programme, where The Archers had given way to *The Record Show* presented by Geoffrey Wheeler.

This appears to have been accepted as a salutary lesson to the programme staff who, for the first time, were now forced to ask themselves if people had simply been listening to The Archers not because they found it fascinating but because it was there. In such hours of need, those involved in long-running programmes often turn to one of the most useful of the BBC's support services, Audience Research. The Archers asked for the audience to be researched. They wanted to know more about the current make-up of the audience. They were told it was two-thirds female, which did not surprise them; that nearly half were under forty-five, which did surprise them; and that three-quarters were working-class, which they did not really understand because of the disagreement over the interpretation of 'working-class'. They wanted to know what were listeners' likes and dislikes. The main likes were facts about the countryside, personal stories, farming matters, comedy, true-to-life quality and

Walter Gabriel. The only measurable dislikes were farming matters and the brevity of the daily episodes.

They also asked for views on the accuracy of storylines involving religion, blood-sports, alcohol and youth, and it is here that the writers and editor were most surprised, not to say shocked. They had long prided themselves on their accuracy but the listeners felt otherwise and gave them a poor rating on all four subjects, with the stories about young people sounding phoney to eighty per cent of the audience. Whoever initiated the research must have been sorry he had ever mentioned it. But these were views that could not be ignored.

Socks were pulled up, and the BBC bosses were happy enough with subsequent scripts to give the programme a lunchtime repeat on the Home Service of the daily episode. This succeeded in winning back some errant listeners and by January, 1965, audience research reports showed that between them, the two daily programmes were getting the same number of listeners as the single, Light Programme edition had back in 1962. It was a considerable achievement in the face of ever-growing competiton from television.

Public relations have always played an important part in the success of The Archers. Most of the cast were constantly being invited to make personal appearances in various parts of the country, and something of an industry had grown up around promoting the programme with newspapers, booklets, books, ties, tea-towels and so on. But one of the things that worried some of the BBC people was that in many of the promotions, other organizations and, even worse, commercial companies seemed to benefit as much from them as did The Archers. For example, not long after a well-publicized visit to Northern Ireland was reflected in the story-line, this news item was broadcast on the Ulster radio and television news: 'Inquiries about holidays here are at a record level, according to the Tourist Board. The Board says that it's had more than 95,000 inquiries from Britain and the Republic since December. This is up by about 19,000 compared with the same period last year. Broadcasts about the Province made in the BBC programme The Archers are one of the reasons given by the Board for the increase.'

That did not bother anyone unduly because there was no direct commercial involvement and because it also reflected the programme's influence. But (and remember these were the days before sponsorship of sport and the arts) there was considerable concern about some of the things that happened when any of the actors or actresses visited apparently harmless agricultural shows. An information officer (not quite the same thing as a public-relations officer,

as becomes obvious) reported to his boss; 'I protested when members
of the cast were photographed using the product, and a panel bearing
the trade name was moved so that it could be seen clearly in the
photograph . . . It seems to me that there are dangers implicit in
these visits to agricultural shows. Public-relations officers, according
to the *Spectator*, are getting slicker and more unscrupulous. Sooner
or later, someone is going to overstep the mark.'

It was the same problem of how far one could go that was also
bothering the writers, as evidenced by this minute from a script
conference: 'Edward J. Mason bitterly complained that The Archers
were not allowed to be provocative, whereas BBC TV seemed to be
given unlimited licence. Chief, Light Programme said that BBC TV
could not be taken as a reflection of the general opinion in the BBC.'

This was a continuing (and continuous to this day) debate, with
the writers always worried that the changing tenor of scripts in television and films would leave them behind, seeming cosy and old-
fashioned. It was, no doubt, difficult for them as members of a
profession that was battering down all kinds of inhibitions and eter-
nally pushing back frontiers, to be part of a group fiercely dedicated,
as members saw it, to maintaining certain standards. The conflict of
interests caused many battles, with the writers seldom winning, at
least as far as the final scripts were concerned.

However, that is not to say that Ted Mason was a man who wanted
the right to be shocking. What he wanted, he said, was 'the freedom
to reflect the world as it is . . . a world that *is* becoming more commercial, that does include vulgarity, that does include sex, that does
include strong language and that does include violence . . . a world
in which values are constantly changing, in which the youth culture
is dominating and in which cosiness plays little part.' But neither
should it be thought that the BBC bosses were old-fashioned or
prudish. They too were tough professionals who knew their audience. They believed that the intimacy of radio created a special
relationship between broadcaster and listener that did not exist
between television and viewer. This also gave them a special responsibility – not to offend or upset the listener unnecessarily. Besides,
they added, a small rural community like Ambridge would not be
hurtling towards the seventies. Life there would be sheltered from
the harsher vicissitudes, it would be much quieter and slower, and
was not that the idyll most of The Archers listeners hankered after?

Ted's retort to that argument was simply to ask how long it was
intended to preserve Ambridge in aspic. But while that is a nice turn
of phrase, it is not consistent with the facts. Indeed Ted himself had,
over the years, had a hand in causing a common brawl which had

resulted in death; in an attempted rape; in an alleged murder; in illicit sex (when it still could be illicit); and in several other violent deaths – all within the confines of his script, of course. Such incidents are not at all consistent with the image of eccentric gentility which The Archers had somehow acquired in the public mind. But was it really odd that Ted Mason should fall into the trap of confusing image with reality? For nearly fifteen years the programme had dominated his life, at times threatening to become an obsession. It was he who had so skilfully blended fact and fiction into so many layers of reality that it is not perhaps surprising he should sometimes fox himself with the blurring of lines.

It was undoubtedly becoming more and more difficult for those involved to be objective about the programme. Was it as good as so many listeners were still saying or was it as awful as some of the critics claimed? To try to find out, the programme heads decided to ask the regional information officer, Kenneth Bird (himself an author and journalist), to study the programme in depth and then to offer a critical assessment. His report was, of course, just one man's view, but it acquires a greater significance because, with the benefit of hindsight, we now know that it was an assessment of the state of play at exactly half-way through the thirty years under review. Here are some extracts:

> Magnetic programmes in radio like The Archers and The Dales preserve the habit of listening. They remind the audience of the existence of radio and of the entertainment and information which it offers. That is why such programmes should be kept in good repair and made to appeal not just to an *existing* audience but also to the changing tastes and attitudes of a *potential* audience. The Archers has many virtues and the fall in its audience over the past ten years hasn't so much been due to endemic faults, but to extension of hours in television and the moving of the omnibus edition from the Light Programme to the Home Service. The Archers has kept to its policy of being *homely*; the people are nearly all *nice*; it offers *escapism* plus a *reassuring reflection* of people's everyday lives with enough action (though this is debatable) to maintain interest. The existing audience is largely uncritical. It seems to like the mixture pretty well as before, although one often comes across the complaint that 'it's a bit slow sometimes' or (in contrast) 'a bit melodramatic'. But the fact that it has an audience of around seven million shows that the customers are fairly satisfied.
>
> But is that enough? Shouldn't the programme be trying to enlarge its appeal, to attract the younger generation?

The Archers is written by middle-aged men. This sometimes shows itself in passages of dialogue between some of the younger characters like Polly, Lilian, Roger and Sid Perks. Occasionally they try a little too hard to be 'with it' – a good example being scenes in which Lilian and Polly discuss the pros and cons of 'going away' with Sean Connery. (This mincing language risks offending older people and making the younger ones openly derisive.)

Naturally, the episodes in a daily serial can't consist entirely of hard plot and character development. Allowance must be made for exchanges of courtesies, chit-chat in fields and at The Bull, although some of the latter are overdone. Leisureliness is a keynote of The Archers, but sometimes it seems *too* leisurely, the pace – perhaps from habit – is *too* laboured. A lot of the dialogue could be improved upon. In one episode, John Tregorran, referring to the quality of the coffee, says, 'The golden good spirits of the old returned master seem to have suffused the whole place,' whereas Woolley calls Scotch, 'a sniff of the old nectar'.

Dialogue and realism wobble still further when *advice* is inserted. An example is the 'sermon' in favour of women wearing spectacles, where Roger, a young man, speaking like an advertising copy writer, says: 'Far too many people go on straining their eyes and having headaches when a pair of glasses would put everything right.'

When it comes to the characters themselves, it seems almost impertinent to criticize established favourites, household names to millions. Even so, I believe that here above all the programme could be improved to attract a wider audience. Take Walter Gabriel. He is a toothless old curmudgeon; his varied hobbies have been entertaining; but hasn't he become a mere eccentric *without* having the background and education to qualify as one? Although he's amusing, he is unconvincing – a caricature rather than a character.

Tom and Ned get good, if superficial, dialogue as a rule. Both are servile and unbelievably benign. Their servility – Tom with his 'sirs', Ned with his 'Master Philip' – belongs to a vanishing era of English peasantry. Isn't this unacceptable to most of our younger listeners? The democratization of the countryside has been going on at varying speeds ever since the war. In the Midlands especially, the lord of the manor is likely to be a successful ironmonger who has to treat his gardener as an equal if he's going to keep him.

In conclusion, let me repeat that The Archers has a job to do – to contribute to the *habit of listening*. To do that it must be compulsive by reason of its colourful characters and its involvement in contemporary life. It must invite sympathy because Ambridge is a gentle relic of Old England, nostalgic, generous, corruptible, and (above all) valiant. In other words, the sort of British community that the rootless townsman would like to live in and can involve himself in vicariously.

Although everyone did not agree with all Kenneth Bird said, he had put his finger on several problems and it was generally accepted that something had to be done. In fact 1966 had not been a good year for The Archers overall, and it was getting worse as the months went by. John Keir Cross's health started cracking and he had to go into hospital, throwing even more strain on to Ted Mason. Then John Woodforde, radio critic of the influential *Sunday Telegraph*, caused a deepening of the gloom:

> There have been signs lately that The Archers is winding itself up for the final curtain. As listeners know and the people of Ambridge do not (a clever device this), efficient plans are being made for speculator Jack Woolley to turn the Midlands village into a large overspill town. It clearly could happen. And where, if it did, would be our daily story of country folk?

That stretched already-taut nerves, especially among members of the cast, who probably did not get as far as the next paragraph:

> There is plenty of time for a reprieve. The script-writers will be careful to follow the real-life technicalities of planning applications and appeals, and actual building need not start for a year. I suspect that the BBC wants to test the strength of listeners' concern, and that if enough letters arrive saying, 'Don't let this happen,' it won't. The story line could be played either way. Some emotional impact is certain if the end of Ambridge as a rural village becomes imminent. A joke to the occasional listener, mannered and contrived with its farming hints, The Archers yet wields a remarkable holding power for almost anyone who tries following the story.

The actors and actresses have always been more affected by the ups and downs of a long-running programme, partly because, being one step removed from the management, they have little control over their own destiny. Some of them take the downs badly, not realizing, of course, the dangers of a self-fulfilling prophesy if they allow it to affect their performances. So when it was announced that, in another re-organization of the radio services, the evening episode was to be taken off the Light Programme and switched to the Home Service, which itself was to become the new Radio Four – it was all to happen in early 1967 – morale slumped even further, with many assuming that John Woodforde had had inside information when he had written about 'the final curtain'. Perhaps it is just as well they were not privy to the audience response at the end of the first week of the cross-over. Many listeners were disappointed, for a variety of reasons, but the main one was obviously the 'lovey-dovey talk' between Carol Grenville and John Tregorran which, many claimed, made them sound more like 'a couple of love-sick teenagers' than their 'mature and usually outstandingly sensible selves'. It may have been for this reason that some listeners suggested that the personalities of one or two of the characters were being changed by the scriptwriters. A sizeable group considered that there was too much farming propaganda and they apparently agreed with the listener who claimed that Philip's visit to the conference at Oxford gave the impression that the programme was being used as 'a mouthpiece for the Ministry of Agriculture'.

Somewhere along the way, Ted Mason had clearly won some ground in his continuing campaign to reflect the real world, because one of the current story-lines was about the pregnancy of the unmarried Jennifer Archer. As his more circumspect colleagues would no doubt have predicted, this did not go down too well with some of the audience: Jennifer's pregnancy had 'spoiled the whole character' of the serial, according to several, who disliked the seamier side of life intruding into the community of Ambridge: it seemed to them 'a drastic innovation' and a handful complained that it made unsuitable family listening ('what with gambling dens, take-over bids, adultery and unmarried mums, Ambridge is not improving'). On the whole, however, the majority were still reasonably happy:

> There were plenty of events and new developments to sustain their interest, they said, and it was clear that the forthcoming marriage of John and Carol was generally approved of, as also was the ending of Valerie Woolley's affair with Ralph Bellamy ('so glad she decided to return to the man she chose to marry'). The scenes concerning Jennifer were 'beautifully handled' by the scriptwriters, it was frequently declared, and the conversation between her and the vicar was especially warmly praised.

Incidentally, the praise was added to by Baroness Serota in a House of Lords' debate, during which she said that Doris Archer's acceptance of the illegitimate baby had represented a 'sensitive and courageous step' by the BBC.

Shortly before that debate, The Archers had received another savage blow with the death of John Kier Cross. As well as being a sad

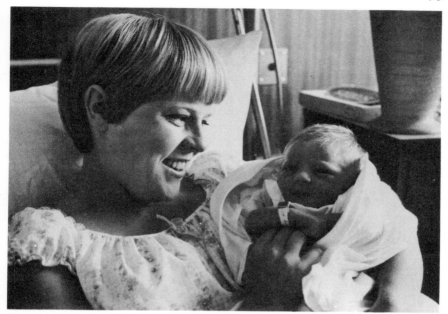

Angela Piper (Jennifer) and her son Benjamin, whose birth coincided with that of Adam in the programme.

and personal loss, John's death served to underline the weakness of the programme's day-to-day support structure, which left the writers, editor and producer vulnerable to almost anything unexpected. It was clearly time for a change. Neither Godfrey Baseley (already two years beyond the BBC retirement age) nor Tony Shryane were actually on the staff. Tony had, in fact, been on a series of temporary contracts almost since the programme began and was, therefore, never in quite so strong a position within the organization as a staff producer. The first step, then, was to bring him on to the staff and once that happened he was given full responsibility – and thus full authority – for every aspect of the programme. To the outsider, that might not seem like an important change, but it was. Without someone in this position, there is always the element of confusion caused by people playing off editor against producer or producer against editor. It had certainly happened in The Archers.

With administrators unaware of his age (probably because of his enormous vitality), or choosing to ignore it, Godfrey Baseley was invited to continue, but with a new contract as script-editor to allow him to concentrate completely on the quality of the writing and the development of story-lines. This, too, was more important than it might appear because it would bring a sharper focus to a vital area of the overall production.

Finally, it was also agreed that the number of scriptwriters be increased to three, as soon as possible. In the meantime, the priority was to find a permanent replacement for John Keir Cross. Some months earlier, Norman Painting (who had played Phil Archer from the very beginning) had been asked if he would like to be regarded as a stand-by writer and had then written some scripts during John's illness. He was offered the contract, which he accepted on the understanding that he could continue to play Phil. The BBC agreed but hinted heavily that he would have be careful how he handled his own character and that they did not expect to see the part increasing.

The new-style team was complete and fighting-fit, determined to engender new interest in the programme, and by the end of 1968 they had succeeded and another corner had been turned. Fan clubs started to flourish. There had been such a club at Bradford University, now there was a new one at East Anglia University (whose members said they particularly liked 'the high moral tone' of the programme), one in Wales, two in the Home Counties and an umbrella body calling itself The Ambridge Appreciation Society, dedicated to 'enjoying the high standard of writing, acting and production'. Then came a little note that also helped raise morale: 'You may be interested to know that Lord Fraser of Lonsdale is one of the most ardent of our Archers addicts. At the weekends he stops in bed until he's heard the omnibus; when he is in South Africa his chauffeur has the duty of sending him a weekly letter reporting the developments in Ambridge.'

International interest was also high, with Radio Botswana joining the long, long list of organizations either broadcasting The Archers or translating it into their own language. It was a vintage year that warmed the programme team and gave them belief that effort is always rewarded.

The same cannot be said of 1969. It started badly (with the news that many overseas countries had dropped the programme) and got worse as death and illness shook The Archers once more. Monte Crick, who had taken over from Harry Oakes as the second Dan Archer in 1961, died after a very harrowing illness; and then Ted Mason was rushed to hospital with a stroke.

In the traditional, show-must-go-on style, Edgar Harrison took over the key role of Dan Archer, and Brian Hayles, a sculptor-actor-turned writer, replaced Ted. Luckily Ted's stroke did not prove too serious and he was soon back to supplement the writing team.

But if the show did go on, it did not do so in the same way. The effort of recovering from body-blows in itself causes problems, sapping energy and enthusiasm. Just how groggy the team was is reflected in their reaction to a pamphlet called *Cruel Britain*, which implied that the programme condoned cruel practices on veal farms. Because of its very nature and considerable influence, the serial had long been the target for complaints and had often come in for much abuse. The complaints, whether or not justified, had always been dealt with courteously, and the abuse had been taken on the chin. But on this occasion, the jibe from an animal-welfare group (not the RSPCA) proved too much. Solicitors were consulted, a stiff legal missive despatched:

> Your published statement about The Archers occurs in the phrase
> – *Report on the veal farms which The Archers say do not exist.* I understand that The Archers programme has never said or hinted that veal farms managed in the manner you describe do not exist.
>
> It must be damaging to the programme for it to be associated wrongly with your attack which you label with the words 'cruel Britain'. Accordingly, I am instructed to call on you either to justify your allegation against the programme or to withdraw it.

The leaflet was withdrawn. But though it restored the reputation of the programme, it could not have done much for the morale to see how unusually sensitive was the programme-team. The end of the swinging sixties must have come as a blessed relief.

CHAPTER 5

The Ambridge Chronicles 1960–9

compiled by William Smethurst

1960

At Brookfield, Dan was recuperating slowly from the injuries to his leg, and Jack gave a lot of help with the livestock. Dan offered to buy Wynford farm (now up for sale again) and go into partnership with Jack – but Peggy refused to contemplate being a farmer's wife again. Eventually Phil bought Wynford's – as an investment for the future – and let the land to his father. He said he was getting restless working for Charles Grenville, who interfered with his work more than he ought to have done.

It was a year of ups and downs for Walter Gabriel. He tried to help his neighbour Mrs Turvey by felling a tree in her garden, but it landed on top of her garden shed and smashed it. He then bought the field next to Mrs Turvey's garden – Parson's field – for his pig venture with Ned Larkin. Mrs Turvey complained to the health department, and Walter was told he could not keep pigs unless the land were properly drained. Walter's bus service also ran into difficulties. After a minor accident (in which Doris cut open her head), Grenville accused Walter of being incapable of driving. Soon afterwards the Education Authority cancelled Walter's school bus contract.

Grenville gave Arkwright Hall to the village as a community centre, and Doris was appointed to the General Purposes Committee. Grenville took Carol Grey out to dinner, and she told him she was an orphan.

In June, Carol called on John Tregorran in his new antique shop in Borchester and saw a painting which shocked her terribly. She recognized the room in the picture, but could not say where it was. A week or so later John told her he had solved the mystery – and also the mystery of Carol's background. He said Carol's mother and father (unmarried) were both artists, but parted when Carol was two. She was then adopted by her mother's cousin James and his wife, who were killed in the blitz. It was Carol's mother, Beatrice, who had painted the picture of the room.

In the summer, which was rainy, cool and stormy, Tom and Pru moved into their new cottage built by Grenville, and Dan discovered his poultry had fowl pest. They were all destroyed and he decided not to keep poultry again.

Paul Johnson caught chicken pox early in the year, and later lost four hounds when he hunted the Ambridge pack. (Reggie Trentham, the Master of Hounds, was laid up with a bad back.) The hounds were discovered, dead, by Tom Forrest. They had canine virus hepatitis. Paul's bad luck continued when his mother, who lived in Bour-

Christine Johnson (Lesley Saweard) with her horse Midnight.

nemouth, withdrew all her capital from his business. He refused to let Chris sell any of her horses, and obtained extra finance from an investment trust called Octopus Ltd. When he signed the final papers he was astonished to find that the man behind Octopus Ltd was Charles Grenville.

In the autumn Tom and Pru considered fostering a child, and visited a children's home where they saw a little boy called Johnny Martin. Johnny started to visit them for the occasional weekend.

Everbody took their holidays late. Dan and Doris went to Torquay, where Dan sat on the beach worrying about Brookfield, and Phil and Paul went off together to Paris, where Paul bumped into a girl called Marianne Peters. Phil was alarmed when he later saw Marianne Peters and Paul in Borchester, and Christine was suspicious when she found a letter addressed to Marianne in Paul's office. Paul explained that she was the daughter of an old school friend, and he was helping her to get a job.

At Brookfield, Dan agreed to form a milking co-operative with Fred Barratt and Jess Allard, designed to increase efficiency and cut costs. A new milking parlour would be built.

Phil went to Holland on business with Grenville, and Carol Grey, who also had business in Holland, travelled with them. Soon after they arrived, Phil was taken into hospital with an infected foot, and Carol and Grenville continued without him. When they arrived back to pick him up they told him they were engaged to be married.

In Ambridge, Walter made a pathetic attempt to buy his old farm – now known as Wynyards – back from Phil, but Phil turned him down.

1961

At Brookfield, Jimmy Grange (love-sick for Carol Grey, who had encouraged his guitar-playing) decided to leave the village, much to the annoyance of Dan who was in the middle of setting up Ambridge Dairy Farmers Ltd. The dairy herds from Barratt's and Allard's farms moved to Brookfield in early April, and Dan's store cattle and followers went to Barratt's farm.

Phil meanwhile bought six Jersey cows to start a Channel Island herd on the Grenville Estate.

Jennifer came back to The Bull after a school holiday in Switzerland, and Peggy was startled to find a letter in her room from a man called Max – presumably a ski instructor. The letter made it clear that sixteen-year-old Jennifer was pretending to be eighteen. Max then arrived at The Bull, and turned out to be Max Bailey from

Charles Grenville (Michael Shaw) and Carol Grey (Anne Cullen) celebrate their engagement.

Wolverhampton. Peggy liked him but Jack refused to let him stay the night.

In March, Ambridge was hit by vandalism. Three teenagers on motorbikes started a fire in a hay-filled barn on the Grenville Estate. Walter Gabriel and Sally Johnson caught them in the act and in a scuffle Walter was kicked about the head and left unconscious. Grenville then arrived and broke one of the vandal's arms with a judo blow.

In court, Grenville said the vandalism might have been prompted by an article he had written for the *Borchester Echo*, which called for the return of corporal punishment in cases of juvenile delinquency.

Tom and Pru decided to foster two boys who were close friends at the children's home, Peter Stevens and Johnny Martin. At Brookfield, Dan took on a new farmworker, Nigel Burton, who immediately upset Doris by asking for a key to his bedroom door. And after Walter had a 'small' win on the football pools, Nelson Gabriel reappeared and persuaded his father to invest three thousand pounds in a light engineering business.

Paul reluctantly allowed Christine to sell some horses when his own business ran into new difficulties. After trouble over a tractor deal and a flaw in the accounts, he offered his resignation to Octopus Ltd. Grenville told him to soldier on.

Reggie and Valerie Trentham's little girl Hazel contracted a mild form of polio, which prompted a widespread immunization programme in the area. She was unable to act as flower-girl at the wedding of Carol to Charles Grenville. Not long after the wedding, Doris persuaded Carol to go to the WI and be nominated as a member of the committee.

In November, Jennifer went to Wolverhampton to stay with Max and his family, and Walter bought an eight-speed bicycle in Hollerton for £30. He decided to go into the junk business on the space next door to the pet shop.

At Brookfield the combined dairy effort appeared to be working well, and Dan installed a bulk milk tank with a 250-gallon capacity.

Phil again returned to his passion for cine photography. He and Jill made a 16mm colour film with sound commentary for the Ambridge Cine Club.

In December Mrs P was suddenly taken ill in London, and Peggy went to look after her.

1962

Carol Grenville was scarcely back from her honeymoon before she was reminded of an old friendship – a bundle of love-letters, written to her by John Tregorran, was found at the market garden. She told John she never meant to abandon the letters, and would keep them for their sentimental value. A week later, however, the Grenvilles' house was burgled and the letters stolen. Both she and John received threatening phone calls demanding £200 for the letters. Carol told Charles Grenville about them, and he was very understanding. By arrangement with the police, John Tregorran dropped £200 at a predetermined spot, and PC Bryden caught the crooks – estate worker Harry White and his accomplice Chuck Ballard.

In February, Jess Allard died and his son Joe decided to sell the farm. After a long discussion, Fred Barratt and Dan approached Phil and asked if he would be interested in taking it on. Phil resigned from the Grenville Estate and joined Ambridge Dairy Farmers Ltd. He and Jill moved into Allard's Farm – which they renamed Hollowtree Farm – and Grenville paid for the redesigning of the kitchen as a parting present to Phil.

The move was not, however, universally liked. Jack complained bitterly because he had not been given the chance to take Allard's over, and Laura supported him. She asked Dan if she could buy an option on Brookfield for Anthony William Daniel when he grew up. Dan refused, and told her not to stir up trouble.

In June, Jennifer entered a dairy queen contest at the Borchester Young Farmers' Club, and told Peggy and Jack that she was going abroad on holiday with Max. They decided there was nothing they could do to stop her.

Lilian was causing less of a problem. She spent the summer doing odd jobs – trying to make five shillings a week to buy hay for her pony, Pensioner, during the winter.

Paul Johnson took lessons as a helicopter pilot, then got a job with a company in East Anglia. He and Christine moved to Newmarket. But a few weeks later, Christine had a bad riding accident and Doris had to go and look after her.

Sally Johnson married Reggie Trentham's old racing chum Toby Stobeman, who took over a new betting shop in Hollerton.

In August, Dan gave Nigel Burton the chance to continue to live-in at Brookfield, or have £4 a week extra and find his own accom-

Richard Todd opens the Ambridge Fête in 1962.

modation. Nigel decided to stay on – partly because of Doris's cooking.

A big step was taken at the beginning of September, when Phil, Dan and Fred Barratt decided to amalgamate the three farms into Ambridge Farmers Ltd. At Hollowtree, however, Phil maintained his special interest – pigs. He bought two sows, four gilts and a boar from Grenville's herd and started to build up a pig unit. Meanwhile Grenville had taken on a new manager, a good-looking Scotsman called Andrew Sinclair.

In the autumn, a new face appeared on the Ambridge scene, when Reggie and Valerie Trentham left the village and sold Grey Gables Country Club to Birmingham businessman Jack Woolley. Woolley described himself as a self-made man and said he was going to turn Grey Gables into an exclusive holiday centre for tired business executives. In a car accident in November he broke his wrist and sprained his ankle, but a week later he was asking Grenville to sell him twenty acres at the bottom of Lakey Hill for a golf course.

Laura took Peggy a seed pearl necklace for her birthday, then broke down and said she was frightened by a prowler outside her cottage. Peggy suggested that she ought to take a lodger.

On 13 December Carol Grenville gave birth to a boy. He was named Richard Charles.

1963

In Ambridge, as in the rest of England, there was an exceptionally severe winter. Snow which fell on Lakey Hill in December was still there in mid-March. Dan had a difficult lambing, after many ewes had been lost in January, which was the coldest month of the century.

The weather had not frozen John Tregorran's heart, however. He fell in love with pretty, blue-eyed district nurse Janet Sheldon and asked her to marry him. She agreed, and they fixed a date in June.

Doris bought an old picture from Walter Gabriel's new junk stall in Hollerton, and Walter bought himself a steam engine. He brought it to Ambridge and called it 'Gabrielle' but soon decided to re-christen it 'Sarah' after an old girl-friend.

Later in the year, Christine and Paul returned to the village. Phil agreed to let them live in the old Wynford's farmhouse if they would renovate it themselves.

Nelson wanted Walter to go and live with him in Borchester. He sent his father £10 and told him he now had a girl-friend whose parents were wealthy and influential in the engineering world. He was surprised and displeased when Walter refused to leave Honey-suckle Cottage.

Janet Sheldon and John Tregorran were married, and had their wedding reception at The Bull.

At Hollowtree Farm, Phil and Jill argued about the schooling of the twins. He wanted them to be privately educated, using money left to him by Grace, but Jill thought they should go through the state system.

Jack Woolley said he was enjoying life away from the big city, but could not entirely subdue his business instincts. He bought the shop next to John Tregorran's in Borchester, and opened it as the New Curiosity Shop. Phil sold Wynford's to Grenville, after he agreed that Christine and Paul could continue living in the farmhouse.

It was a busy time for Ambridge Farmers Ltd. In the spring they signed a sugar beet contract with the Kidderminster factory, and spent £800 on a precision drill and down-the-row thinner. After a cool, wet summer the harvest was better than expected, with crops above the ten-year average.

Dan and Doris went on holiday to Guernsey, and Jennifer started a teaching course at the West Midland Training College in Walsall.

At Grey Gables a young Brummie called Sid Perks turned up and warned Jack Woolley that his barman was on the fiddle. Woolley saw in Sid a younger version of himself, and sensed that he could make a success of life if he were given the right opportunities. He gave Sid a job as his chauffeur and right-hand man.

Ambridge also won the Best Kept Village competition, and Jack decided that Ambridge now had more tourist potential. He and Peggy started planning to build a new dining-room at The Bull, overlooking the bowling green.

On 31 October, John Tregorran was with Carol when she received a phone call to say that Janet had been killed in a car crash, and Charles was badly injured. He had been driving Janet home to Blossom Hill Cottage. Surgeons at Borchester General Hospital operated on Charles, and amputated one of his legs.

Jennifer returned home from college, and brought Max with her for the opening of the Cellar Club. Jack agreed to let him stay overnight at The Bull.

At Christmas Tom arranged a concert to raise funds for the old folk, and Nelson was furious when he heard that Walter was working as Father Christmas in a Borchester store.

1964

A busy New Year for Walter Gabriel. Agatha Turvey forced him to leave the Hollerton Pet Shop (he was not pulling his weight in the partnership) and he started breeding maggots in a shed near her garden. She complained to the Parish Council, and John Tregorran forced Walter to abandon his scheme. He then went into partnership with Jack to buy a balloon from a Mr Snout of Hollerton, and called it Pegasus. He sold his granny's chamber pot to John Tregorran for £15, and, still wheeler-dealing, bought a stuffed gorilla from a man in Felpersham. He called it George, and said he needed it as a sign-post for a new junk shop he was opening in Ambridge.

In the spring, Jack bought Jennifer a moped so she could return home from college more often. Both he and Peggy were worrying about the cost of the new dining-room at The Bull, but their problem was solved when Laura gave them a present of £25,000. (She later increased the amount to £30,000.) They decided to build a self-contained flat over their dining-room extension, and asked Laura if she would like to live in it. She said she would be delighted.

New people came to the village. Twenty-three-year-old Gregory Salt started work at Hollowtree Farm – he came from a farming family in Heydon – and PC Albert Bates replaced Geoffrey Bryden as the Ambridge constable.

Valerie Trentham returned unexpectedly with Hazel, and said that Reggie had died in the Bahamas. She and Hazel stayed at The Bull.

In April, Grenville had the first fitting of his artificial leg, but did not return to Ambridge until the summer. Paul Johnson gave up being a helicopter pilot and Grenville offered him a job running a small agricultural machinery firm owned by Octopus Ltd.

At Hollerton Fair, young Sid Perks had trouble with some lay-about acquaintances from his past who stole his motorbike and embarrassed him in front of his new girl friend, twenty-one-year-old Polly Mead, the barmaid from The Bull. The motorbike was later found abandoned half way to Birmingham.

It was a year of consolidation for Ambridge Farmers Ltd. Dan bought some sheep-handling equipment he saw at the Royal Show, and Christine worked in the farm office at Brookfield for a few weeks but did not enjoy it very much. At Hollowtree Farm, Jill was upset when Elsie Catcher, the village schoolmistress, told her that Shula was a backward child.

August was warm and dry, and the harvest was excellent. After much persuasion from Fred Barratt, Dan and Doris went on holiday to Malaga.

At Grey Gables, Jack Woolley decided to go on a six-month cruise, and had the brilliant idea of asking Valerie Trentham to run his guest house for him. She agreed, and it was decided she would try to build up the stables again with the help of Lilian Archer.

The village was astounded when Charles Grenville went to America, alone, after telling Carol he was disposing of his majority interest in Octopus Ltd. Paul Johnson desperately tried to raise the finance to buy the agricultural machinery firm he was running. Jack refused to find the money for him.

At Christmas, Doris was given a Jack Russell terrier by Dan, and called it Trigger. Walter played Long John Silver in the vicar's production of *Treasure Island*. He had a real parrot.

1965

In January, Charles Grenville phoned Carol and said he wanted to settle permanently in America. Carol flew to see him in New York, then returned to Ambridge to sell up the estate. A few days later she heard that Charles had collapsed and died, struck down by a bug he picked up in the East, which had lain dormant for years. In his will he left the house and three companies to Carol. The estate was sold, on Richard's behalf, and bought by Jack Woolley and Ralph Bellamy (the son of Admiral Bellamy, who had died recently after running a large estate next to Ambridge).

The barmaid at The Bull, Polly Mead, turned down a proposal of marriage from Gregory Salt, and accepted one from Sid Perks. Sid, however, became jealous when she got a job at the Regency Hotel in Borchester, so she broke their engagement off.

At Brookfield, Doris decided to lean to drive a motor car, and insisted that Dan and Phil try to teach her. Eventually she gave the idea up, and bought a pony and trap.

Walter Gabriel gave his parrot from *Treasure Island* to a certain Mrs Twelvetrees of Felpersham, and then bought an elephant. She was called Rosie, and before long had a baby called Tiny Tim.

Doris organized a party of WI members to go on a four-day trip to Holland, and on 31 May represented Ambridge WI at a Buckingham Palace garden party. In the summer Dan, Doris and the Barratts went on holiday to Ireland. While they were there, Brookfield was burgled and Doris's collection of copperware was stolen.

John Tregorran returned home after a long holiday in Spain (where he spent some time in hospital after trouble with his vocal chords) and took a leading part in organizing the Ambridge summer festival. It included a pageant depicting the Garden of Eden. Walter's

Doris (Gwen Berryman) talks to Dan (Monte Crick) from her pony and trap.

elephant Rosie, and Tiny Tim, were a huge success. Walter, however, had another problem on his mind. He had learned that Nelson had forged somebody's signature on a cheque. The matter was hushed up with difficulty.

It was a wet, miserable year on the land. The hay crop at Brookfield was almost a complete failure, and at corn harvest, barley was poor in quality and wheat yields were low. Fred Barratt told Dan he had had enough of farming and wanted to retire next Lady Day. Phil and Dan therefore agreed to pay off his interest in Ambridge Farmers Ltd by instalments, and Fred sold his land to Laura, who rented one hundred acres back to Phil and Dan.

Laura was having a busy year. She moved into the flat at The Bull, and was saved from a nasty car accident by a handsome, dark-haired young man called Roger Patillo. She gave him a job as her chauffeur, and he soon became friendly with Lilian. When Jennifer came home she suggested that he should start a folk-singing group in Ambridge.

Jennifer herself was in disgrace at home, having been thrown out

Roger Patillo (Jeremy Mason) and Lilian Archer (Elizabeth Marlowe).

of her flat in Walsall after a rowdy party. She was back in favour, however, when she had a short story published in a magazine.

In November, Roger Patillo confessed to Laura that far from being a suspicious foreigner (as Jack thought), his real name was Roger Travers-Macy, and his family had money and breeding. They were also cold and indifferent, which was why he had chosen an assumed name. Laura was taken aback, but grateful when he gave her a good tip for the stock exchange.

Woolley bought a large topaz brooch for Valerie Trentham, and persuaded her to become engaged to him. Later, he was delighted to discover that Grey Gables had been owned by a Sir John Woolhay three hundred years ago, and that a branch of the Woolhays later became known as Woolley.

Christine and Paul adopted a little boy called Peter, who was born on 5 September.

1966

The year began badly at Brookfield, when Dan slipped a disc while trying to move a heavy tractor wheel. A few weeks later a fire broke out and destroyed a tractor and damaged the house. The police were called in and found evidence of arson. More fires broke out in the Ambridge area, and the village was in a high state of nervousness throughout the spring. The police finally caught the arsonist setting fire to The Bull: he was Frank Mead, Polly's father. He was admitted to the county hospital for nervous and mental disorders.

Sid comforted Polly, and she agreed to become engaged again. The wedding was fixed for September.

Life was quite busy for the Gabriels. Walter found forty-two gold sovereigns in an old cash box hidden up the chimney of his cottage, and Nelson went into partnership with Reggie Trentham's old racing chum, Toby Stobeman. They opened a casino and betting shop in Borchester, much to the delight of Jack, who discovered a taste for gambling.

Woolley and Valerie Trentham were married, and Carol and John gave them a pair of bedside reading lamps. Roger Travers-Macy (who was becoming increasingly friendly with Lilian) went to work at a Borchester bookshop, and Laura engaged a Miss Fairlie as her chauffeur/housekeeper. When John Tregorran opened a Borchester bookshop of his own, he took on Roger Travers-Macy as his assistant manager.

At Brookfield, some hay was lost because of thunderstorms, and Phil agreed to increase the sheep to 150. They decided to make a sheep wintering yard with straw bales that year. Farm worker Paddy Redmond (a piano-playing Ulsterman who had failed to qualify as a vet), started going out with Nora McAuley when he was on holiday in Belfast. He brought her back to Ambridge and she got a job as barmaid at The Bull.

Woolley gave Sid Perks the job of managing Arkwright Hall Recreation Centre (where he planned to build a swimming pool that could be converted into a dance hall in winter). He also organized a grand summer fête at the Hall which turned out to be a disaster. Many villagers stayed away, and accused Woolley of pretending to be the squire of Ambridge.

John Tregorran again proposed to Carol (the first time was in 1954) and this time she said 'yes'.

On 27 September Sid and Polly were married. Jennifer and Lilian were bridesmaids, and wore pale blue brocade dresses. Polly was given away by Jack. The honeymoon was spent in Cornwall, and afterwards Sid and Polly returned to the flat at Arkwright Hall. Woolley took on a new chauffeur called Higgs.

It was a difficult autumn for Peggy. Jack gave her a wrist watch after a spectacular win at Nelson's casino, but later she saw from his cheque book that he had paid £450 in gambling debts in one week alone. She also discovered that Jennifer was secretly going out with Nelson Gabriel. When confronted, Jennifer said she would go out with whom she pleased, but Nelson himself suddenly became elusive. Walter became worried when Jennifer questioned him about his son's whereabouts.

Jill told Phil she was expecting a baby, and Jennifer told Lilian that she was expecting one as well. Lilian was shocked, but promised to stand by her sister.

Both Walter and Nelson disappeared. Zebedee Tring claimed he saw them heading for Southampton.

1967

In January, Jennifer told the vicar she was pregnant, and asked him to speak to her parents. He told her to tell them herself. When she did, Jack tried to throw her out of The Bull, but Peggy would not let him. The pregnancy became the talking point of Ambridge, particularly as Jennifer refused to name the father. Walter Gabriel – back from a fabulous cruise with Nelson – became convinced that Nelson was the guilty man. He was shaken still further when Nancy Tarrant from Penny Hassett visited him and said Nelson had made *her* pregnant. He told her to move out of the district and promised to send her money.

On 1 February, John Tregorran and Carol were quietly married in Ambridge parish church. John sold the bookshop in Borchester, and they bought Manor Court for over £20,000. John soon joined Laura in forming the Ambridge Protection Society, aimed not at Nelson Gabriel, but at a vast village development scheme planned by Bellamy and Woolley.

Woolley – prompted by Valerie – cut down the famous yew trees in front of Grey Gables, and the Protection Society made its first protest. Woolley, however, had other problems to worry about. The Arkwright Hall Recreation Centre was proving a failure. He told Sid and Polly it would have to close, and they would be out of work.

At Brookfield, Paddy Redmond the dairyman complained because Phil would not introduce a milk bonus scheme, and decided to work for himself. He quarrelled with Nora at The Bull, left Ambridge Farmers Ltd and headed south.

In May, Nelson was reported dead. The police said he was travelling in a light 'plane which crashed into the sea. Walter's confusion was made worse by inquiries from the French police about his son's business deals.

Jill gave birth to a daughter, who was immediately rushed to hospital with a heart condition. A surgical examination showed a narrowed valve into a main artery, and a hole between two large pumping chambers. The baby, named Elizabeth, underwent an operation to widen the pulmonary valve.

In the wettest May for two hundred years, Sid Perks tried his hand at farming, taking a job at Hollowtree Farm. But he soon fell out with Phil and left to work for a Mr Brown at Paunton Farm (outside Ambridge). Mr Brown then revealed that his pig-farm activities were just a cover – he and his brother were professional gamblers hiding from a gang of thugs demanding protection money. Sid left and went to work for Paul Johnson, who was now running the garage.

On 22 June, Jennifer gave birth to a baby boy, and decided to call him Adam. She also heard that a novel she had written had been accepted for publication. Leaving hospital, she went to stay with Laura for a while, who said she knew the father of the baby was Paddy Redmond. Jennifer did not deny it.

The police raided Paunton's Farm after a mail-van robbery, and said fingerprints found on an empty scotch bottle were identical with prints taken in Nelson's luxurious Borchester flat. Was he still alive? Walter said 'his Nelson' would never be so heartless as to fake his death and break his father's heart. Jack Woolley offered to help with money for the defence when Nelson was tracked down, and other friends clubbed together to buy Walter a tropical fish tank, with fish, to help cheer him up.

In the autumn, Woolley found out that Valerie had been dining alone with Roger Travers-Macy on several occasions. He told Carol Tregorran that he and Valerie were drifting apart.

Phil won a newspaper competition with an essay about 'Farming in the Future' – the prize was a world tour of farms in America, Canada, Australia and New Zealand. Jill told him he must seize the opportunity and that she would look after Hollowtree while he was away.

Dan returned home to Brookfield one night and found the house ransacked. Doris was lying at the foot of the stairs, unconscious, and was taken to hospital. She had been knocked down by an intruder making his escape.

1968

Doris soon returned home from hospital, and claimed damages from the Criminal Injuries Compensation Board. The Brookfield attackers had knocked her out and she had broken her wrist.

Phil meanwhile left the country on the first leg of his round-the-world farming tour, and Nelson returned to England having been tracked down by Interpol. Borchester magistrates heard evidence that he had visited Paunton's Farm the night before the mail-van robbery, and had been referred to as 'boss' by Charles Brown. He was committed for trial at the Assizes, and moved to Gloucester gaol. Walter visited him in prison, and Nelson said he had been framed. Walter was convinced of his son's innocence.

At the Bull, Jack gave Peggy his winnings from a session at the Borchester Casino: £245. She later found him unconscious in bed, nursing an empty whisky bottle.

Confident that the Woolley/Bellamy Ambridge development scheme would go through, Paul Johnson planned to expand the garage by adding a coffee bar. Sid, working as a forecourt attendant, shared his enthusiasm. In March, however, the development scheme was defeated, and Laura held a celebration party.

Nelson also had something to celebrate. He was found not guilty, and freed without a stain on his character. He took Walter off on another cruise.

Doris was pleased to receive £250 from the Criminal Injuries Compensation Board.

It was a romantic summer. Lilian met a Canadian Air Force pilot, Lester Nicholson, who was in England on an exchange course, and quickly fell in love with him. She told Jennifer that her affair with Roger Travers-Macy was over. Jennifer knew this, however, because Roger was already asking her out. Gregory Salt started work again at Brookfield, and became engaged to Nora McAuley.

It was also a wet summer, the wettest since 1931. At the beginning of July multi-coloured dust, believed to be of North African origin, was brought down in Ambridge (and the rest of England) by heavy rain. Dan's barley was damaged by thunderstorms, and the quality of grain proved to be poor.

At The Bull, Peggy was relieved when Jack developed a craze to own a boat, and bought one with Walter. They kept it on the River Severn, and Peggy hoped it would keep Jack's mind off gambling and drinking.

Phil returned from his world tour, and told Jill he thought

Greg and Nora Salt (Gerald Turner and Julia Mark).

Ambridge Farmers ought to be more progressive, and Dan ought to think of retiring.

There were two new arrivals in the village: Hugo Barnaby, a cousin of John Tregorran, arrived from America and helped John with one or two deals in the antiques world; and David Latimer, the new vicar, moved into the parish. Tom liked him, but was made uneasy by his free and easy ways, and refused to call him by his Christian name.

Polly Perks won £1,000 on a premium bond, and used it as a deposit to buy the village shop. It was found that Sid could not be the sub-postmaster because of his past criminal record.

Lester Nicholson was invalided out of the Canadian Air Force with ear trouble, Roger Travers-Macy proposed to Jennifer, and Valerie walked out on Jack Woolley.

There were more periods of heavy rain in September, and Dan found the cows loose at Brookfield, with one sinking into the slurry pit. He jumped down to save it and another cow fell on top of him, badly bruising his shoulder. The accident was blamed on Greg Salt, who had quarrelled with Nora and left a gate open.

In the autumn Jennifer got a teaching job and moved to Brookfield for a few weeks so that Doris could look after Adam during the day. Dan was presented with an illuminated address by the NFU to mark forty years faithful and active service to agriculture, and Paul Johnson was warned that his garage business was going bankrupt through bad debts.

Two weddings closed the year: Jennifer married Roger Travers-Macy, and Nora McAuley married Gregory Salt.

1969

As the year began, Dan was beginning to find it increasingly difficult to cope with full-time work on the farm. It was a very wet spring – made particularly serious because heavy rains the previous autumn had delayed the drilling of winter wheat. Dan struggled to get his barley drilled, even though the ground was in bad condition. He finally succumbed to a severe chest infection, and was taken to hospital. Phil and Doris both urged him to retire, but Dan refused. He was allowed home, but was ordered to report to hospital twice a week for treatment.

In February, Paul was forced to sell his garage business to Bellamy. Sid continued to work as the forecourt attendant, and refused to help Polly in the shop. He changed his mind, however, when she told him she was pregnant.

Jill decided to stand for the Rural District Council, and campaigned against the threatened closure of Ambridge village school. Much to her surprise she was elected, and became Councillor Archer.

When Dan was fit enough to travel, Bellamy offered him the use of his villa at Torquay for his convalescence. Dan and Doris accepted gratefully, and Jennifer and Roger moved into Brookfield while they were away.

At The Bull, Peggy was having a bad time with Jack, who was drinking harder than ever. She discovered that he had called in a firm of valuers to look at The Bull. A bright spot, however, was the marriage of Lilian to Lester Nicholson – known as 'Nick' – on 26 May, and further good news when Anthony William Daniel – known as Tony – finished his farm institute course and returned to Ambridge to work for Bellamy.

In early summer, Polly and Walter were attacked in the post office by a thug who tried to snatch money and postal orders. Polly grappled with him, and as a result had a miscarriage.

Paul Johnson set up a small firm to develop his own patented automobile equipment, and persuaded a large motor company to provide extra finance for his research. Walter also went into a new line of business: he got permission to open a short-stay caravan site on his land, and called it The Old Mill Piece.

Things seemed slightly better at The Bull, when Jack began to take more interest in the place and suggested opening a 'Playbar' with fruit machines and expresso coffee. Peggy was dubious, but agreed in the hope of providing Jack with something to do. The 'Playbar' was opened, and heartily disliked by most villagers.

Tony bought himself a scooter, and started going out with the vicar's daughter, Tessa Latimer. Soon, however, he startled Peggy by saying he wanted to emigrate.

On her birthday, Doris was given a wrist watch by Dan, and twelve pullets by Walter. She lost eleven of them when a fox invaded their pen, and kept the other as a pet. Dan finally went to see his accountant and solicitor to discuss his retirement, and subsequently announced that he had made up his mind to go into semi-retirement. After a family meeting it was decided that he and Doris would move to Glebe Cottage, and Phil and Jill – and the children – would move into Brookfield.

Carol Tregorran gave birth to a baby girl, to be called Anna Louise.

As the year came to an end a group of youths ran wild in the Playbar, and Peggy was warned about disturbing the peace by Ambridge's new policeman PC Drury.

CHAPTER 6

The Countryside

by Phil Drabble,
Adviser on Country Matters to The Archers

Tom Forrest and I are much the same vintage, and we have lived our lives in similar circumstances, and seen the Midland countryside and its wildlife change in many ways since we were lads.

My father was a doctor, and farmers who were his patients gave me the freedom of their land. I grew up – like Tom – with a good ratting dog and a bagful of ferrets. The local squire, too, was a hospitable man, who believed all young men should be taught country ways, not by schoolteachers, but by gamekeepers who were skilled in their traditional arts.

Other patients at my father's surgery were also skilled in 'traditional arts' – which included the art of poaching rabbits and pheasants without getting caught by the keepers!

So I had a foot each side of the fence and could calculate both ends of the equation before I could say my twelve times table. And Tom and I have seen habits and fashions and even the face of the countryside change out of all recognition in the course of our lifetime.

Fifty years ago, the head keeper was one of the most influential men in any village. In those days, work was a dirty word to the aristocracy (unless done by other people) and their estates were managed by land agents, many of whom robbed their clients blind. The landowners had so much time on their hands that sport was their most important preoccupation, and their head keeper's job depended on the quality of sport he could provide for his master and his guests.

There was nothing scientific about the job when Tom started work on Squire Lawson-Hope's estate. Field sports were wrapped up in tradition and gamekeeping lore was handed down from one generation to the next. Almost any creature which was not classed as game was an enemy of game by most keepers' standards, especially birds with hooked bills and animals with canine teeth. Foxes and hedgehogs, stoats and badgers, owls and hawks were all 'controlled' by trapping, or snaring, or shooting, or poison as opportunity offered. Straying cats were all assumed to be 'wild' and even the wife of the head keeper where I grew up had to keep her beloved pussy on a collar and chain because that was the only safe place on her husband's beat.

When this was the policy of all neighbouring keepers on estates that covered huge tracts of land, like the Bellamys' and the Lawson-Hopes', the effect on other wildlife was dramatic. Not only pheasants and partridges benefited from an almost total lack of predatory enemies. Song birds did too. When Tom and I grew up there were more thrushes and blackbirds and linnets in the countryside than there are now because there were fewer hawks, owls, stoats and weasels to prey upon them. Partly because so many birds were common, nobody thought anything wrong with taking eggs and, like many boys of my generation, I first became interested in natural history when I went ferreting in winter, or birds nesting in spring and summer.

When I was about twelve, I discovered the nest of a barn owl ('white owl' we called it) in the hollow of a pollarded willow and decided to collect an egg. Our natural history master actively encouraged us to collect eggs and insects, knowing I suppose that once we got the fever, we would always be keen on country things. The only unbreakable rule he made was that we should never take more than one egg from a clutch, so that at least we did minimal harm.

I was acutely aware that owls can be vicious birds in defence of young because I knew a keeper who had lost an eye as a result of neglecting elementary precautions at the nest of a tawny owl. So I decided that the safest way to collect my egg was to make sure the hen owl was unlikely to launch an attack. I took a friend with me, who could be trusted not to blab where the nest was, climbed up the willow and caught the sitting owl by her wing butts when she raised them in threat. Long experience with keepers had taught me that most birds held by the base of both wings are immobilized so that they neither come to any harm nor inflict any.

My young friend was far greener. Instead of reaching up behind the owl to take her wings from me, he put his finger within reach of her talons and discovered, to his cost, that birds of prey are extremely uncomfortable to shake hands with. She drove her talons into his flesh till she held him by the finger bone. He yelled and shouted blue murder till I feared he would arouse the neighbourhood, which was the last thing I wanted to do as we had no right to be there and the owner was known to wield his stick with a heavy hand. So I loosed the bird's wings and she, in turn, loosed my pal so that she could fly to a vantage point from which she had the choice of retreating or defending her eggs as necessity demanded. It drove the lesson home to me that considerable skill is necessary to handle any wild creatures!

By keeping my ears open I often discovered precisely what the keepers' plans for the evening were and if they were all going to be down one end of the estate, putting up pens for the pheasants or doing some job that demanded team work, I used to call on some of my father's other patients and tip them the wink. They often took the opportunity of poaching a few rabbits on the part of the estate which would be free of keepers – and they often invited me to join them as a reward for feeding them the information.

I have always loved being in quiet places at night. It was vital to keep quiet, so that nobody suspected our presence and, if you keep quiet enough, even wild creatures forget your presence too.

Running a long net out and pegging it every few yards, so that it stands erect and firm enough to stop rabbits at full speed, is very skilled work which I was not allowed to try for years. So I used to be left at the nearest vantage point to whisper a warning if anyone came along. It was an ear-stretching job, because capture, in those days, could mean seven days' prison for poaching. A field mouse rustling through the grass at my feet sounded like a squad of coppers. An owl, flying by on utterly silent wings, made just enough cold draught to convince the most unimaginative that ghosts not only exist but come out to haunt boys who are wicked enough to go poaching.

Most youngsters, I suppose, love the masochistic pleasures of scaring themselves and those boyhood days – or nights – with poaching friends are as vivid now as then, and often form the basis of a story in Tom Forrest's Sunday morning chat.

When I was not with poachers or keepers, I spent a large slice of my holidays with a professional rat-catcher. His skin and clothes were the same colour as the earth. Indeed, both were impregnated by years of grime so that his natural camouflage was as perfect as a wild duck sitting on her sedgy nest. He moved as smoothly as a cat and it was instinctive for him never to make a silhouette against the skyline. If you went out with Hairy Kelly, casual onlookers would assume you were alone.

Another lad had been out with us, one day, and he had come home with a young rat, hardly ready to leave the nest, which he hoped to rear and keep as a pet. An elderly relative, who disapproved of us going ratting on Sunday, insisted on taking us to evening service. All went well till half way through the sermon when the air was rent by an agonizing whisper from young Mac. 'Quick, quick,' he cried. 'My rat's going down the central heating duct.'

He had it nestling for warmth and security in his pocket but, when it had got over its initial shock, it had made a bid for escape. A successful bid, as it turned out, because, once it had gone to ground, it preferred the security of the cold ducting to the uncertain warmth of its new owner's pocket.

Newts are among the creatures which were more common then than now in the Archers countryside and I have always been especially fond of them – 'wet efts' or 'askers' they were called in our parts. As children, we kept them in aquariums in spring and watched their exotic courtship, when the flamboyant male, with gaudy yellow spotted belly, curved his body round the female and she produced strings of eggs, like sausages, breaking the end egg from the string with her delicate 'fingers', to wrap it separately in the leaf of a water plant, where it lay hidden from predators (including the male newt!) until the tadpole hatched out.

We fed the adult newts well on earthworms so that they thrived and waxed fat when, instead of being uncomfortable, they split their skins and wriggled out of them as delicately as if they had been fairy gloves, to appear, resplendent, in a bright, brand new skin.

When we had had our fill of watching them, we returned them safely to the pool where we had caught them – and at Home Farm Adam and Debbie still do the same today.

While we were catching newts, in the old days, my keeper friends were catching vermin. Spring, between the end of the shooting season and when the pheasants laid in April, was the time when keepers settled old scores. They laid out lines of tunnel traps, each designed to look deceptively secure, as a refuge from pursuit, but each containing a trap that waited, with infinite patience, for an unwary foot to spring it. The traps were examined daily so that, while doing his rounds, each keeper got to know almost every animal and bird that shared his beat.

I used to love to accompany any keeper who would tolerate me and my fund of knowledge gradually grew as odd snippets of country lore were passed on. When Tom or George Barford talk about wildlife and country ways, they often echo the stories I heard in those days.

One chap I went with was a wizard on the weather. He said he could smell rain at the end of a drought and I really believe that he could. The arid air does seem to grow softer and usually a little cooler as the change approaches, just as there is nearly always a cooling wind immediately before a thunderstorm. He had odd beliefs about cows lying down before rain and swallows flying close to the ground. And he was a fervent believer that mistle thrushes were not known as storm cocks for nothing. When one was piping on top of his oak tree, nothing would persuade him to go on to his beat without a sack to put over his shoulders.

After the war, everything in the Archers' countryside changed. The numbers of gamekeepers were decimated by their employers and vermin proliferated in the years when sport took a back seat. The conservation movement gathered momentum too, so it not only became impracticable to control vermin as in the past, but it also became socially unacceptable.

The first wild badgers I ever saw were on the beat of the old head keeper who had taken me in hand as a boy. He would have turned in his grave if he had known what was there, but his boss's son, who had come into the estate, was delighted and showed them to me with pride. I have badger-watched scores of times since and am always intensely careful to make no sound, check that I am downwind, so that they do not get the taint of human odour and to pick a spot where my silhouette does not give away my presence.

That first night, we were walking through a woodland, chatting quite loudly, when we heard a crashing in the undergrowth. There seemed to be as much row as if a herd of cattle had broken into the wood, so we stopped dead in our stride to locate the source of the noise. Within seconds a pair of badger cubs rolled out of the undergrowth locked in what looked like mortal combat. They rolled and gambolled, not in anger but in play, and I watched, spellbound, etching on to my mind the details.

But the most remarkable thing, in retrospect, was not the pleasure I got from watching badgers playing but the change in attitude between generations of landowners. The new owner had only a couple of keepers whom he kept on more as a charity to old family servants than for the useful work they did, and he was as interested in what went on on his estate out of the shooting season as he was in actually shooting pheasants.

The change was being reflected everywhere after the war, and was caused partly by new rearing methods. When Tom Forrest started as a gamekeeper he spent long weeks in summer with rows of coops, each housing a broody hen and sixteen or seventeen pheasant chicks. But new owners with progressive methods, like Charles Grenville and Jack Woolley, changed all that. Nowadays pheasants are reared intensively, like domestic poultry, with never a foster mother in sight. The eggs are hatched in incubators and the chicks are raised in heated brooders, surrounded by wire netting which keeps pheasants in and predators out. Even when the chicks are big enough to be put out in the woods, they are kept for weeks in fox-proof release pens, from which they only wander when they are old enough to fly into the trees to roost in safety.

So there is really no need, now, to slaughter every possible enemy of game, because wire netting and electric fences keep the victims safe anyway. There are still a few bad keepers and status-conscious syndicate shooters who encourage them to get the best returns for their money, at whatever cost to wildlife. But on the whole sportsmen are no longer the enemies of wildlife they once were.

There is a debit side. Song birds no longer enjoy the fringe benefits of living on a great estate. There are now more crows, magpies, jays and stoats to steal their eggs and eat their chicks. As in human society, when discipline flags the baddies thrive. I was watching a pair of crows trying to get a leveret for breakfast, just after dawn, one day and it was impossible not to be impressed by their low cunning.

Hares have their young above ground instead of in burrows, as rabbits do. They usually have four leverets which they drop in an open nest, sometimes on bare plough and sometimes in a clump of nettles or feggy grass. The leverets are born fully furred, with their eyes open, and the greater the danger that threatens, the stiller they lie. They can run within an hour or so of birth but obviously not fast or far enough to escape a crow or fox or stoat. So, for the first few hours, they mostly avoid being eaten by relying on their marvellous camouflage and keeping absolutely still.

When they are about twenty-four hours old, the doe hare disperses them to a number of nests, or forms, scattered perhaps a hundred yards apart. If, by bad luck, a predator does find one, at least he does not also find the rest. The odds against catastrophe falling on the whole litter have climbed to four to one.

Cunning crows do not rely only on luck to stumble across the defenceless leverets. The morning I was out, there was an old carrion crow perched on the topmost twig of the highest tree in the area. He had a grandstand view of everything that went on around him and he was waiting for sitting ducks and pheasants to leave their nests to feed and drink. Watching where a sitting bird comes from is the easiest way of finding her nest, as every countryman knows.

One of the snags of dispersing a litter of leverets is that it is necessary to make the whole rounds to suckle them – and the crow was aware of that too. The doe left the youngster she had been feeding in a nettle clump and hopped a hundred yards to feed another. The crow took the cue and flew down to inspect the nettles. Quick as a flash, the old hare returned and dashed at her enemy with feet flying. One good kick from her powerful back legs could lay out a bird much bigger than a crow, so that there was apparently no chance of getting near the first item on his menu. But as if by telepathy, his mate then joined him and, while one of them flustered the hare by flying at it to tempt it to retaliate by chasing it away, the other nipped in and grabbed the helpless leveret. Fortunately, dispersal saved the rest – at least temporarily.

In the years that Tom has been at Ambridge there have been tremendous fluctuations in the populations of rabbits. Before 1953, rabbits were part of the English countryside and, although they may have done a lot of damage, many small farmers, on marginal land, relied on selling trapped and ferreted rabbits as part of their income.

The arrival of myxomatosis changed all that. It is one of the foullest diseases imaginable and I find it impossible to conceive of the state of mind of anyone who will spread it deliberately. The first waves spreading through the country wiped out a very high percentage of our native rabbits, often up to ninety-five per cent where they were most thickly populated. For the first time in my life, I could be in the country for half a day without seeing the familiar sight of rabbits feeding and playing and making love.

Their absence had unexpected effects. Everyone had realized that rabbits ate grass and farm crops and garden flowers, but it had not been so obvious that they also ate the seedlings of wild trees, gorse, brambles and other plants that would, without the rabbits, have grown up into thick scrub. When they went, the face of the countryside changed within a few years. Open spaces suddenly grew dense thickets of cover which helped the pendulum swing back.

The disease did not wipe out all the rabbits either, and they have a marvellous breeding mechanism that helps them through such crises. They mate as soon as their young are born and the embryos begin to develop immediately. If there is plenty of food about, it is obviously wasteful to rear only a small litter, so the female rabbit reabsorbs the young into her system, comes into season and mates again immediately, hoping to produce a larger litter next time.

Having spent a great deal of my youth with dog and ferrets, I know from experience that in dry weather, especially frosty weather, rabbits love to 'lie out'. That is to say they squat in tussocks and other thick cover above ground in preference to going to ground, where there is often uncongenial company – with fleas and other uninvited guests.

But I had not realized until the lack of rabbits produced so much new top cover just how fond rabbits are of lying out. Quite suddenly a new race of what countrymen labelled 'bush rabbits' appeared which never seemed to go down a burrow but spent their lives above ground.

It was nature's marvellous contribution to the rabbits' self-preservation. The plague is spread mainly by rabbit fleas which breed in the weatherproofed warm litter of rabbit warrens and which cannot survive the rigours of the out of doors. So, by forsaking the burrows and camping out in the newly-grown thick cover outside, there is far less chance of one rabbit with the disease infecting others which are now less likely to share the same fleas.

Although it is illegal to spread myxomatosis, clever scientists are now trying to develop a super strain of the plague to prevent the rabbit population regaining its footing in the countryside. A great many countrymen, including me, hope that they do not succeed.

The population of other creatures fluctuate more naturally as a result of changing weather conditions. Ambridge is as well a wooded countryside as my own home, a few miles away, has always been. I have spent countless happy hours sitting quietly in a leafy English wood just waiting for things to happen. Our wood, at home, is grand habitat for woodpeckers, and the green woodpecker, or yaffle, is one of my favourite birds. He has a wild, demonic call that chases the echoes round the trees as if some madman were splitting his sides with laughter.

Yaffles feed by getting grubs and other insects from the nooks and crannies in the bark of trees and, if there are wood-boring beetles, their chisel bills can strip and chip away the wood until the tunnels of the beetles are exposed. Woodpeckers have remarkable tongues which literally fold away in their bills so that, when unfolded, the tongue is considerably longer than the bill that houses it. But such a long and delicate tongue is exceptionally susceptible to cold and, in hard frost, it is not uncommon for woodpeckers to get frostbite of the tongue when they are exploring frozen crevices for food. The really bad winters of 1947 and 1963 caused a dramatic crash in the numbers of yaffles in the woods.

There are always swallows round the homes of Tom and me

because we both live in pretty isolated spots. I did once manage to persuade a small colony of house martins to nest as well, which look very like swallows except that they do not have the chestnut breasts and there is a conspicuous white spot on top of their rumps which make them look like butterflies as they are flying away. The other main difference is that the swallow's tail is forked into two distinct streamers, which float behind it, and the house martin's forked tail appears to be 'webbed'. Swallows nest inside buildings and martins prefer to build their mud nests under the eaves. This makes them favourite targets for house sparrows which fly up to the basin-shaped martin nests, dispossess the owners and lay a clutch of their own eggs there instead.

The snag with both Tom and me is that we both have so much stock about that there is always a colony of sparrows living on the crumbs that fall from our poultry's table and the poor martins never get a proper chance. So my martins gave it up as a bad job and moved to less disturbed quarters.

Swifts, or Jack Squealers, have similar pointed wings to swallows and martins, though they forego their attractive colours for a dusky brown. But I do not believe that any bird in the sky can fly better than a swift. It flies so well that it literally sleeps and mates on the wing and, if it lands on the ground, its wings are so long and pointed and its legs so short, that it cannot always get airborne again. However, the most marvellous thing about swifts is that, when the fledglings first leave the nest holes under the eaves, they never return nor are they fed by their parents. They know by instinct how to catch flying insects and, even more marvellous, they know where to go to migrate for the winter. Young swifts that have been caught at their nests and had numbered rings put on their legs by birdwatchers have been recovered in Africa a few days later, in spite of the fact that their parents do not migrate for some weeks.

But the change in the ways of keepers that has given me the most pleasure since The Archers was first broadcast is undoubtedly in their attitude to predators. I have already mentioned the reduced manpower on the estates, limiting the work that can be done, and also the virtual factory-farming of pheasants, which enables the birds to grow up in safety. But that does not explain it all. There are now ten bird watchers to every one when Tom and I were young, and the keepers and conservationists have discovered that they have far more in common than either ever imagined. Keepers and naturalists talk much the same language, though they still have different priorities.

I know that I have been able to convince keepers that badgers, in which I happen to be very keenly interested, are not the villains they are painted. I had hand-reared badgers at complete liberty in my wood for five years or so and now there are wild badgers in artificial setts I have constructed so that I can observe them closely.

Many keepers treat scientists with a certain amount of suspicion. I do myself because I share the keepers' view that too many boffins pontificate from the centrally-heated comfort of their laboratories. But my keeper friends were interested in some of the experiments I did with my badgers because they could see for themselves that they were practical as opposed to a load of theory. One of the things that impressed them most was the fact that, although I had badgers always working in my wood, it contained more pheasants than surrounding keepered territory.

What gave me the clue was a broody bantam that had laid away and was sitting on a clutch of eggs within a few yards of the badger sett. In the ordinary way, I should have moved her but I showed her to a keeper friend and left her to see how long she lasted. She went quite safely until the eggs were within twenty-four hours of hatching, when the chicks had begun to cheep, partly as a signal to the others to start chipping at the shells, so that they would all hatch more or less simultaneously, and partly so that the hen would grow accustomed to their individual voices and accept them as 'hers'.

The badger must have heard the cheeping too and gone to investigate when, of course, he found the sitting hen. A fox would have marked it, like a pointer dog, and pounced, and that would have been that. But the badger must have simply nudged it, to see what it was, and it flustered off the nest, squawking so loudly that it roused me from my bed. It was a brilliant, moonlit night and I could see the white hen clearly, squatting and squawking in the paddock below the bedroom window. The badger followed up to investigate but, instead of pouncing, he nudged it again and away it flew. The pursuer was getting more excited now and followed closely, but he did not close in to kill and I managed to arrive on the scene in time to rescue the hen.

Left to himself, I am sure the badger would have killed the hen when she eventually got stuck in the hedge bottom or a bramble, and good luck to him if she was silly enough not to use her wings to escape. Certainly, if the same thing had happened to a pheasant, she would have flown up into the nearest tree and I am sure that, where there are badgers foraging in the undergrowth, it makes the pheasants roost aloft, safe out of the way of foxes, which are far more dangerous. Many modern keepers now take the civilized view that there is room in the countryside for other attractive creatures as well as game and they are far more tolerant than they used to be.

The changes in the countryside in the lifetime of both Tom and me are by no means all for the worse!

The Seventies

CHAPTER 7

The Archers' Story III

by Jock Gallagher

The new decade offered the chance of a fresh start. Wondering how the latest re-organization of BBC services would affect them, Tony Shryane and Godfrey Baseley faced up to the seventies in self-questioning mood. The new blueprint, *Broadcasting in the Seventies*, ended the regional services and promised a new look for the national radio networks. How would The Archers fit into the re-styled Radio Four? In a blueprint for their own future, *The Archers as Radio Entertainment in the 1970s*, they asked themselves if there was still enough material and interest for there to be further mileage in telling the everyday story of countryfolk. That was a fundamental question, the kind asked only when one has confidence in the answer:

> The answer to this is yes. But it must be appreciated that over the years, very great changes have taken place in the whole pattern of rural life and that this is likely to accelerate over the next few years. No longer is it possible to think in terms of roses round the door and quaint old village pubs and 'gaffers' sat on the bench outside. The whole status of village life has changed, particularly in those villages within an hour's journey by motorway from a big urban area, and these changes should be reflected in the programme in a more positive way. Although the population has changed, the problems and pleasures associated with rural life are still very much with us. In fact, looking at the village as an entity, it could well be

described as a microcosm reflecting the life of any group of people whether urban, surburban, or market town. A new social structure has established itself, divided roughly into three parts: (1) the native; usually manual workers or small farmers, (2) the newer population with an urban background and (3) the bigger, more progressive farmers and land owners. The only 'snob' or class distinction element, if it exists, stems mainly from the more urban section because of their lack of awareness of a traditional code of conduct and etiquette. There are plenty of human problems, relating to age, health, youth, social life and administration. Legislation, of any kind, and its enforcement is resented particularly on questions of right of way, building, planning, etc. 'Keeping up with the Jones' is now very much a factor of village atmosphere. News and gossip continues to be a 'natural' part of the community. The traditional village 'bobby' has been replaced by a much more mobile policeman equipped with up-to-date means of communication and covering a much larger area. The village shop now has a touch of the 'supermarket' about it. The local doctor is now part of a group and it is the same with the vet. The district nurse is more highly trained and equipped with a car and covers a wider area. The village baker, butcher, shoe mender, carpenter, saddler and blacksmith have disappeared or operate as mobile tradesmen. The small farmer is rapidly disappearing. Nevertheless, listeners enjoy hearing various characters reminiscing about life in the village twenty or thirty years ago, and this can be done quite naturally with such characters as Dan and Doris Archer, Tom Forrest, Walter Gabriel, Zebedee Tring, Jethro Larkin.

The document went on to pose a number of other questions and present firm answers. Should The Archers continue to span a broad canvas or narrow its scope to one section of the Ambridge community at a time? The answer was to continue with a broad canvas, but giving specific stories top priority for periods of time, rather than handling a number of issues at once. Should the programme concentrate more on the ever-growing Archer family? Yes, was the reply, because the family now comprised several distinct and diverse units, spanning many interests and occupations. Moreover Phil should take on the role of father figure, with Dan and Doris moving into a different but undiminished role. Finally, was the balance of sixty per cent entertainment, thirty per cent information and ten per cent education still the right one? Here the answer was to add a slightly stronger – but always relevant – documentary flavour, exploring a range of issues from social and political to economic and

Editor Godfrey Baseley (left) and Bob Arnold, who plays Tom Forrest (centre) check up on country lore.

administrative, but without reducing the programme's entertainment value.

So it was to be a shuffling of the cards rather than a new pack; the new age would lean heavily on the experiences of the past. Changes there might be, but only after due caution. This attitude suited one of the new programme heads: 'The Archers is a valuable BBC property. It is especially important at the moment that it should maintain its hold on the radio audience as the schedule patterns change. If, in order to ensure this, we have to make radical changes . . . then we must not fear to do so, only remembering that any proposed breath of change in connection with The Archers is inevitably accompanied by melodrama of monumental proportions.'

The inherent danger in this kind of situation is that caution can lead to equivocation, which can lead to over-caution. Confidence ebbs away and everything becomes much too tentative. This inevitably happened with The Archers and the programme lost its way. One story-line – the kidnapping of Jennifer's son, Adam – stretched credulity to breaking point, and the memos started to fly:

That we are in trouble is now becoming very obvious to our most loyal and keen listeners, particularly those who have always appreciated the accuracy and authenticity of the programme. If this situation is allowed to go on for much longer, I shall find it very difficult to justify the programme as 'a reflection of the social and economic life of the countryside' when I talk to the BBC Agricultural Advisory Committee.

As the concern increased, there was, for the first time, serious consideration about taking the programme off the air. For nearly twenty years it had been outstandingly successful, but now, said the programme bosses, it sounded undeniably tired and the latest audience figures showed a slight drop in listeners to the evening edition and a bigger drop for the Sunday omnibus. Would it not be better to stop before the programme altogether lost its grip on the audience? Nobody answered the question. Instead, Tony Shryane and his colleagues were desperately trying to pull themselves out of what seemed like a dizzying decline in their fortunes. But Ted Mason's health was delicate and he was far from his best form. And then when they decided to play up some of the younger characters, the actor who played young Tony Archer went down sick and was out of action for a month. Almost as if it were the final kiss of death, the usually-eager agents became more reticent about making their artistes available for recording sessions. Luck had deserted The Archers. The five-thousandth episode had been celebrated in style, but it looked as if there would be no twentieth anniversary party.

There was, indeed, no party when the anniversary came round in January 1971, but few believed the explanation – that it had been decided to wait and make a really big splash on the twenty-first anniversary. The new year was little more than a month old when the programme received the most shattering blow of all, the death of Ted Mason. For all of its twenty years, Ted had been the sheet-anchor. In a tribute, the programme head, wrote:

> Whatever the problems, Ted had always been there with those beautiful scripts that sometimes delighted the audience, sometimes reduced them to despair and always gave them enjoyment. He has transported listeners to a rural idyll with all its pleasures and he has brought them to tears with stories like the tragic death of Grace Archer. And whichever it was, he did it with style. His total dedication was never doubted though it was sometimes taken for granted. His contribution was immeasurable.

Ted's loss was also immeasurable, in both personal and professional terms. His death left the programme without any real sense of direction. From Godfrey Baseley's original sketchy outline, Ted – with the help of Geoffrey Webb and the other writers – had created a whole community and for twenty years he had guided the destiny of the Archer family, of Walter Gabriel, Tom Forrest, Sid Perks, Jack Woolley and all the other good folk of Ambridge. What would now become of them?

At a later script-conference, Godfrey Baseley said he felt a re-examination of the programme's purpose was necessary. But while this found unanimity, there was disagreement about how to make progress, and before any resolution was found, there was yet another blow – the death of Denis Folwell, one of the original cast who had played Jack Archer.

Was the pack of cards, re-shuffled for the seventies, about to collapse? Again, before that question could be considered, along came another event, but this time one to lift the depression, at least for a little while. It was a visit by Princess Anne, to the BBC's new Pebble Mill studios in Birmingham which housed The Archers and about seven hundred other personnel. After officially declaring the building open, the Princess's tour would include a visit to the studio to watch the programme in production. When the time came, it was a great moment for the cast and production staff as they were presented to the Princess. It was even more of a thrill to Gwen Berryman when she gave Princess Anne a gold medallion that had been specially struck to mark the golden wedding of Dan and Doris.

That occasion and the twenty-first anniversary, now just around the corner, allowed at least an outward show of confidence, lifted morale and brought The Archers back into the public eye. In private, however, the gap between Godfrey and his new bosses was not getting any narrower, with Godfrey obviously feeling more and more bitter because he sensed his long experience was being ignored. At one stage, he wanted to make his point by having his name removed from the list of credits broadcast at the end of the programme. He was talked out of that, but no one was apparently able to persuade him to attend the anniversary party. He simply sent a telegram of good wishes to the cast. Norman Painting spoke for everyone when he said later: 'We were naturally surprised and disappointed.' It should have been Godfrey's night, after all the party was to celebrate twenty-one years of his creation. It was like a parent missing his child's coming-of-age, but he was so upset that he did not want to risk spoiling the party for the others. It underlined that a very sad parting of the ways could not be far away.

In a memo to London, the Birmingham programme boss wrote:

'Godfrey, as you know, is a very forceful character and it is sadly clear that we cannot encourage him to our way of thinking. After nearly eighteen months, we are still looking in different directions.' When it was later decided that Godfrey's contract would not be renewed, a memo said: 'The final decision was, to my mind, mutual.' From his comments to the press, Godfrey did not agree. He was quoted in *The Times* as having been dismissed without warning or consultation, and with news of his departure having become public before he had been officially informed.

That Godfrey Baseley, creator and, for twenty-one years, the driving force behind the most successful radio programme ever, should leave The Archers in such a way was very, very sad. It would be nice to now reveal that the breach has since been healed, but it has not. Despite invitations to subsequent events, Godfrey has not been back to the studios since 1972.

The gap left by such an enormous personality was not easily filled and it was three months before a replacement was found. The new editor (who, it was announced, would also write some of the scripts) was Malcolm Lynch, until then editor of television's most successful soap-opera, *Coronation Street*. In recognizing his abilities as a drama-

Anthony Parkin, who took over as agricultural adviser in 1972.

tist, the BBC also acknowledged his urban background by supporting him with Anthony Perkins's appointment as agricultural adviser.

Malcolm Lynch's brief was to change the style and direction of the programme. 'To pull it back from the brink of disaster,' he was told. He had before him a report on audience response which cast doubt upon 'the realness and credibility of the serial, which is perhaps strengthened by the fact that many former listeners have stopped listening because they find the programme dull and the characters and the story-line unreal.' Malcolm set to with gusto. The winds of change positively blasted through Ambridge as drama and realism became the order of the day. The audience were first shocked and then resentful and their violent reaction recalled a warning from an earlier boss: 'any proposed breath of change . . . is inevitably accompanied by melodrama of monumental proportions.'

At the next script-conference, Malcolm conceded that the first wave of the new look had gone a bit too far. Someone complained that the use of strong language created an abrasive atmosphere, while someone else admired the undoubted increase in realism, through the quality of the writing. Someone said that it would be better for characters to be angry about situations rather than angry about people and someone else said that there should be a balance between abrasion and peacefulness. What everyone agreed was that things could be toned down a little, but not too much, because for the first time in several years, the audience figures had actually increased.

As the shock-waves subsided, the programme undoubtedly improved. At a meeting in London, it was said that the previous Sunday's omnibus had been the best for some years: 'The general feeling was that there had been a great all-round improvement . . . more action, better dialogue and, in particular, a rather better way of using farming material.' Any thoughts of taking off the programme were now dismissed and all the old confidence returned. But then fate dealt yet another nasty blow. Malcolm Lynch's health started giving out. The strain of his enormous efforts to change the direction of a great institution was too much and after less than a year in the job he was forced to give up and retire to the peace and quiet of the West Country. He has since regained his health and resumed his writing career. The programme team meanwhile were back where they had started, without an editor and with the writing team once more reduced to two.

There was yet another three-month gap before a new script-editor could be found. The new man, Charles Lefeaux, was another urban dramatist, a former actor and radio drama producer who lived in

Hampstead. But, with Tony Parkin very successfully looking after the agricultural content, Charles brought a new calmness to Ambridge and steadily built on Malcolm Lynch's success. And he began in earnest the search for new writers to strengthen the team. When he recruited first Kerry Lee Crabbe and then Keith Miles, he issued his manifesto for The Archers in the second half of the seventies.

Our programme is intended as entertainment – it is primarily about people, and about the country way of life. It takes place in an agricultural setting and should reflect rural events and new developments in farming, but it is no longer intended to be an information programme. As Controller, Radio 4, says, 'Plugs for any cause whatsoever are out,' and we must be very careful not to become heavy-handed when agricultural and country things are discussed. Audience research reports continue to show that two thirds of our regular listeners are working class, over fifty per cent are over fifty, and the majority are women. Over twenty-five years in the trade have taught me that this kind of audience demands above

Left to right, Philip Garston-Jones (Jack Woolley), Colin Skipp (Tony Archer), Julia Mark (Nora Salt) and Bob Arnold (Tom Forrest) in the studio, 1971.

all what they consider to be reality – not of course *ciné verité* but what they can accept as real people in real situations.

The secret and the power of all successful soap-opera is that it provides the customers not only with an escape but also with characters with whom they can identify and because it is an escape they need the stability of old friends going about their business year in and year out. As one perceptive customer put it: 'Characters, events, situations and places carefully enmeshed in a network of plausibility and reality built up over many years.' Without over doing it we must, I think, keep characters who have left Ambridge or who haven't appeared for some time alive by references – perhaps Walter should get a letter now and then from Nelson, and we certainly must guard against the introduction of new characters who are quickly disposed of and who sink leaving no trace.

The really serious thing that emerges from the recent Audience Research report is that between 1968 and 1972 there has been an astonishing drop from seventy-seven per cent to fifty-eight per cent of those who can accept that The Archers are true to life. We must therefore above all create in our scripts people our listeners can believe in and stories and situations which arise from character, not letting our situations batter the characters till they are unrecognizable. We have our abrasive characters – Laura, Woolley and Grundy – and all should not be eternal sweetness and light among the others; they must not be too cosy, and like the rest of us, they can be irritable and have their quarrels, but these should be properly motivated and not occur in every scene of every episode.

The Radio Four Controller, Tony Whitby, underlined this approach:

Times have changed. There are now many outlets for information on radio. Informational programmes are popular these days in their own right. Indeed, the audience for *You and Yours* is now pretty competitive with that for The Archers. It follows that the right place for propaganda and useful information is in programmes designed for that purpose and not in programmes such as The Archers which are designed for entertainment. This isn't to say, of course, that we are wrong to take great care to get our farming facts right and to reflect new developments and rural events fully and accurately. The point is that the informational aspect should be totally subservient to the dramatic intention. It is there *only* to give realism and conviction to the story and the characters.

There now followed a long period of normality during which the programme ran on an even keel. Memos between those involved were civilized, if somewhat dull. Script-conferences concentrated on developing story lines and recorded the success of a trip some of the cast made to the Netherlands (to learn about the EEC) and, with amusement, that the programme was to be used to help Gurkha soldiers to learn to speak English!

The 6,000th episode occurred in 1974 and was duly celebrated; show-jumper Ann Moore joined the cast for a series of guest appearances as herself; two general elections took place and were noted in Ambridge; Tony Shryane, constant as ever, maintained his usual impeccable control over the programme; and, most important of all, the audience seemed blissfully happy and the listening figures stabilized at about three million.

There were changes in management, both in Birmingham and London, without any undue effect on The Archers. Charles Lefeaux continued to strengthen the writing team, recruiting William Smethurst, former journalist and television script-editor, to join Brian Hayles, Keith Miles and Bruno Milna. This was the first time that so many were involved in the writing and it left more time for planning and research. Tony Parkin continued to supply a steady flow of farm-

William Smethurst, who joined the team as a writer in 1975 and became producer in 1978.

ing stories and to keep a careful check not only on the detail of the agricultural content but on its balance within the programme.

A minor squall disturbed the peace in 1975, when an agricultural accountant wrote to *The Times* accusing the writers of getting their sums wrong in the winding up of the Bellamy Estate. He said that if Ralph Bellamy sold 2,500 acres and settled the remaining 1,000 acres on his infant son, the tax liability would be ruinous. The reaction was immediate, because the government's Finance Bill was then being debated in the House of Commons, and other newspapers seized on the opportunity to popularize the very complex subject of taxation. Inside the BBC, there was some anxiety. 'Why do you think we have got it wrong?' asked one memo. 'We simply cannot afford to make these kind of mistakes. It wrecks the credibility of the programme, the very foundation of which is accuracy and authority.' Another letter to *The Times* followed:

Sir, I am honoured that my tax problems should merit the attention of your very well-qualified correspondent, Mr Horne. Sadly, however, I have to tell him that he makes at least two false assumptions:
a) that being a country yokel I did not get expert advice and
b) that I intend settling 1,000 acres on my son, James.
My advice from an excellent country accountant has allowed me to net over £1 million (after paying capital gains tax of £225,000) from the sale of 2,500 acres. I intend using some of that to take my family into the sun for an indefinite period. I have no very definite plans for the future but we are not simply turning our backs on Ambridge.

Ralph Bellamy

Sadly, *The Times* said loftily that it did not 'under any circumstances accept letters from fictitious people,' but that if an official of the BBC cared to sign it on Mr Bellamy's behalf, it could, of course, be considered for publication. One did, and it was printed.

The next major happening would be the twenty-fifth anniversary of the programme and with little to deflect them, attentions were now firmly focused on making this the most successful occasion to date. Plans were carefully laid for a very special party, to start on New Year's Eve and roll into the very anniversary itself – a reprise of the first edition of the programme which began on 1 January 1951 with the Archer family wishing each other a Happy New Year. Hints were dropped that a television documentary would be welcome and the writers were sent to their studies to think about some kind of book. Other publicity and promotional ideas were mooted and the storyline for the anniversary programme was discussed in detail.

At the script-conference, it was agreed that there should be a birth to coincide with the jubilee and, as Tony Archer was born the same year as the programme, it was only appropriate that he should be the lucky father. His wife Pat would give birth in the early hours of New Year's Day. Should it be a girl, boy, twins, triplets or even quads? Should it be a difficult birth with the child being born handicapped? What name should be given? As in all the branches of the Archer family, Tony and Pat's firstborn was a boy. Mother and son did very well and the baby took the simple name of John.

A television documentary, *Underneath the Archers*, was shown on BBC 2, the same evening as Radio Four broadcast the anniversary edition of The Archers, and there were also several books to commemorate the occasion. Norman Painting published his memoirs, *Forever Ambridge*. Keith Miles and Brian Hayles both wrote novels; one, *Spring at Brookfield*, was set in the aftermath of the First World War, the other, *An Ambridge Summer*, had a modern setting. A *Who's Who of Ambridge* was also compiled, with pen portraits of everyone who had ever been in the village.

The press were fed numerous stories: 'During twenty-five years, there have been nine scriptwriters'; 'Tony Shryane has produced all but a handful of the 6,500 episodes'; 'While the programme has been on the air, the cows at Brookfield have been milked 26,000 times and between them, the villagers have drunk about 20,000 cups of tea.'

But the story that captured most attention was the re-enactment of the notorious Grace Archer death scene. During research for the jubilee, it was discovered that the scene was missing from the sound archives. Tony Shryane decided to remake it with the same two artistes, Ysanne Churchman and Norman Painting. The press enjoyed that. There were pictures in every paper and millions of television viewers saw it happening 'live' on BBC 1's lunchtime magazine, *Pebble Mill at One*.

Then, as an extra layer of icing on the cake, Norman Painting's contribution to broadcasting – twenty-five years as Phil Archer and writer of more than one thousand episodes in nine years – was recognized with an OBE in the New Year Honours List, and Gwen Berryman, Doris Archer for all of the twenty-five years, was named Midlander of the Year.

Norman Painting, as English as it is possible to be, having been born in Leamington Spa on St George's Day, wrote his first script for the BBC in 1945 and, as he was to do later with The Archers, he also played one of the parts. He later joined the BBC as a producer and reporter, doing talks and interviews and appearing in children's programmes before joining The Archers for its trial run in 1950, and then became an almost permanent member of the cast when it was launched nationally on the Light Programme. He continued with his own writing – poetry, stage plays, radio serials and features – and, as we have seen, was asked to join The Archers writing team after the death of John Keir Cross. With Ted Mason, he was winner of the Writers' Guild Merit Award in 1976 for his part in writing Archer scripts.

Gwen Berryman's award was 'in recognition of the way in which she had made a Midlands life-style the envy of millions around the world'. Gwen was herself born in an industrial town, Wolverhampton. The daughter of a talented musician and sharing her birthday with St Cecilia, patron saint of music, she knew very early on that she too wanted a musical career. At the age of fourteen she left school to become an operatic student and went on to the Royal Academy of Music. There she won a four-year scholarship, took the gold medal for being best singer in her year and was awarded the top diction prize, although she had not even been taking diction lessons. The rules for awarding prizes were promptly changed.

When she left the Royal Academy, she went into the Lyric Theatre musical *Derby Day*, directed by Sir Nigel Playfair, and followed that role with others, including a part in the Gracie Fields' film *Looking on the Bright Side*. But then Gwen was taken seriously ill with pneumonia. After treatment, she had to stay at home for six months. Desperately unhappy, she returned to Wolverhampton and it looked as if her short career was over.

It was at this point that the courage she had shown throughout her life first became obvious. She shrugged off the after-effects of the pneumonia, gave up singing and joined the Salberg repertory company in Wolverhampton with whom she stayed for fourteen years. She combined that work with opening a little shop in the town and the odd bit of broadcasting, and her career was just ticking over steadily in 1950 when she auditioned for a part in The Archers.

In the seventies, Gwen had begun to suffer from crippling arthritis, but had never once missed a recording, although one or two did have to be made at her bedside. For most people – especially coming up to the age of seventy – that would be enough. Not Gwen Berryman. Instead of retiring, she simply carried on, and added to her problems by doing charity work on behalf of other arthritis-sufferers.

With these special honours and all the massive publicity, it seemed that at twenty-five, The Archers was still going strong. Successful occasions are hard acts to follow and, wisely, Tony Shryane and company therefore contented themselves with a quiet period, consolidating their position. But in the constant public glare, there is never time for entrenchment and almost as a result of delayed shock, two or three long-standing listeners wrote in to complain about the recent changes. Immediately, doubts were raised about how far the writers could go in bringing the programme up to date without alienating old supporters. In the self-questioning came another review of the *raison d'être*. Was the shifting balance between farming information and entertainment right for the times? Well, The Archers was now an entertainment which took place in an agricultural community. Yes, but that was no excuse for watering down the agriculture, was it? What about the even more delicate balance between fantasy and reality? Surely the audience wanted escapism? Yes, but they also consistently demanded realism.

At one of the script-conferences, which was attended by Tessa Diamond, the first woman in the writing team, there was a debate that could as easily have been initiated by Ted Mason; it was about reflecting the world as it was. On this occasion there were two bones of contention. William Smethurst said he felt the BBC policy document on the use of trade names was ambiguous, and Tessa Diamond said she felt tied by not being able to write about politics. Proving that life had changed, both received responses that were considerably less dusty than Ted Mason would have expected in his day. The programme head said that the intent on trade names was to prevent advertising but that the writers had a just complaint if that meant their scripts were turned into a kind of Esperanto. They were given room for manoeuvre, although not too much. Then Tessa Diamond was told that the reality of village life was that people did not declare their political affiliations or views, either because they thought them too important to discuss or because they took it for granted that everyone else knew all about them. However, if the storyline made it essential, there was, again, some room for manoeuvre.

It was not quite so easy to answer another problem, however. The realism of the programme was yet again questioned by critical listeners, some of whom said that villages the like of Ambridge no longer existed. Up until now, the writers' Ambridge had been a conglomerate – bits of different villages (particularly Hanbury and Inkberrow) had been used for publicity pictures, for example. There really was only one answer, to pinpoint one village. Coincidentally, the writers were then considering how Ambridge should celebrate the Queen's Silver Jubilee later in the year and so it was agreed that if a suitable village were located, its festivities could be a model for the programme.

The writing and production team in the mid-seventies visit Ashton-under-Hill and meet country writer Fred Archer. Left to right, William Smethurst, Tessa Diamond, Brian Hayles, Fred Archer, Tony Shryane, Keith Miles and Charles Lefeaux.

It was like falling off a log. A story in the *Worcester Evening News* brought the claims flooding in from villages in Worcestershire (always seen as the Archer county of Borset), all insistent that their community was just like Ambridge. A short-list had to be drawn up: Ashton-under-Hill, Birlingham, Clifton-on-Teme, Cradley, Hallow, Ombersley and Upton-on-Severn were added to Hanbury and Inkberrow. After a tour of some of the prettiest villages in England and after much heated discussion – everyone had their own idea of Ambridge – the first on the alphabetical list was chosen. And just as it happened, Ashton-under-Hill was the home of author Fred Archer and his family.

The fun of the chase was shattered by the news that changes in the Radio Four schedules would alter the times of broadcasting The Archers, both in the evenings and on Sundays. The evening move – to five past seven – was bad enough, but the switch of the omnibus, from its seemingly rightful place as a part of the English Sunday morning to 6.15 in the evening, caused 'grave disquiet' to Tony

Shryane and his colleagues. Apart from what it would do to Sunday mornings, it was bound to mean a serious loss of audience. It took a great deal of persuasion for the team to see it as a positive move, not to hurt the programme, but to help build up the Sunday evening figures.

As part of the publicity to highlight the change of time, a new version of the famous signature tune was introduced (it was by a modern group called The Yetties) and the first programme was made in quadrophonic sound on location in Ashton-under-Hill. Breaking new ground did little to soften the blow for the regular Sunday morning listeners. Many of them were furious, some said it was an outrage, a gross interference to an ordered lifestyle, an affront to all things English. Even Dan Archer himself wrote to express concern. (Edgar Harrison, the actor, received so many protests that he wrote a strong plea for re-consideration to the controller of Radio Four.) He was told, 'To assume a loss of listeners because of the new timing is to assume that people have only been listening because it's there. I believe most people listen because they enjoy it and they will do so at 6.15 on Sunday evening. The Archers is healthy and robust and can well stand a bit of movement without suffering too much.'

Another lady, writing on behalf of 'the whole neighbourhood', said she had cried because she could no longer hear the programme. 'It is like losing members of the family.' A more forceful lady from Merseyside insisted that as she could not listen to a forthcoming omnibus, 'you can jolly well send me a brief resumé of what's been going on during the week.' She actually got her resumé, but most of the other complainants had to make do with standard, duplicated replies. (Just over a year later, the omnibus was switched back to Sunday morning, although at the slightly later time of 10.15. A clear victory for public opinion.)

In all the confusion, one might be forgiven for thinking that listeners were more concerned about where the programme was rather than what was in it. But once more the writers were reminded that in bringing the story up to date, they must hasten slowly. In conversation about whether or not she should start a family, the character Betty Tucker had referred to the contraceptive pill. In came the letters complaining of 'indelicacy', 'unnecessary embarrassment', 'offensiveness' and so on. But showing how times had changed, inside the BBC as well, the script-writers were supported by the programme head:

The reference to 'the pill' was very brief and it was in context of a

discussion that seemed to me perfectly acceptable in such a programme, reflecting as it did the embarrassment that many people
still have in talking about these matters. I certainly do not think it
was in any way offensive nor did it fall below the programme's
usual high standard.

With Charles Lefeaux's retirement and – almost unbelievably –
the impending departure of Tony Shryane, it had become obvious
that major changes were going to be needed to maintain the thrust
of the programme's direction. Replacing Charles as script-editor
was going to be difficult enough, but Tony Shryane was unique,
with his long experience of the production and a knowledge that
was impossible to transfer to anyone else. How could he be
replaced? No one underestimated the problem and there was, once
more, consideration of ending the programme, but that gave way
to more positive debate and, rather than rush into the decision
which would affect the whole future of the programme, breathing-
space was gained by William Smethurst becoming caretaker script-
editor. Eventually out of the melting-pot came the resolve that a re-
shuffle of responsibilities was essential. In recent years the staff producer (Tony Shryane) had carried the full weight of the production
under the handicap of the freelance script-editor working away from
the office. This made the essential job of marrying script and studio
performance vulnerable to such things as delayed mail deliveries
and other logistic problems. In future, the staff man would be the
editor/producer on whom the script-editor role would also devolve,
and the freelance help would be used in the studio direction of the
programme. It made sense because it focused all the effort on the
production office and allowed one person to exercise total control
over all the essential elements.

When the picture became clear, it was also easier to see the possi-
bilities of finding someone to take over from Tony Shryane. The
machine was working well because there was still time for a long
hand-over from Tony to any successor. Finally, from the candidates,
William Smethurst was selected.

A thirty-three-year-old former journalist, William had been
working with the BBC in various capacities since 1970. He had
graduated from Lancaster University and worked his way round
the world before he joined the BBC regional news staff as a sub-
editor in Birmingham. He also started to write radio plays and
then moved to television drama as script-editor on the controversial
Play for Today series. He left to become a freelance writer in 1975,
when he joined The Archers' script-writing team. He wrote a

screenplay, *The Young Robin Hood* for the Children's Film Foundation and won an award at the Moscow Film Festival. Another of his scripts, for *The Unbroken Arrow*, was runner-up in the 1977 EMI children's film awards.

Vanessa Whitburn, a drama graduate who had been in the theatre before joining the BBC as a studio manager, also became the new studio director. She had spent the previous year working in Birmingham as a radio drama producer.

While these changes were taking effect, there were two deaths that left the team shocked. Julia Mark, who played the Irish barmaid, Nora, died at the age of forty-nine from a kidney disease, and a few months later Gwenda Wilson (Aunt Laura) died of cancer. She was fifty-five. In an article for the BBC staff newspaper, Tony Shryane wrote about the effects of death on a long-running programme:

> The death hits you on different levels – personally and professionally – but the separate reactions impinge on each other with bewildering speed and almost instantly fuse into a single emotion – despair.
>
> Gwenda Wilson and I had been friends for many years, even before she joined The Archers, twenty-odd years ago. She was a delightful artiste whose infectious gaiety made her popular with everyone and she had that indefinable Australian quality that kept her going at parties when everyone else was beginning to fade. When she died, I could not believe that her energy and enthusiasm would no longer be there to enliven our rehearsals and recordings. But then – and this is where, I think, the real sadness comes in – I had to abandon my personal feelings and decide what to do about the programme and the recordings already made with Gwenda.
>
> It may seem like an easy decision . . . 'The show must go on' is part of our folklore; and somewhere in one's head there's, 'Gwenda would want it that way!' Would she? Or is that rationalization because, in honesty, it is also the easiest way out?
>
> Finally, you do make the decision and the recordings go out. Her voice comes up – as Aunt Laura, the crotchety old busybody of Ambridge. What have you done? That's not how you want Gwenda to be remembered. Then – and perhaps again it's rationalization – you realize you're straying from the narrow line between soap-opera fiction and real-life fact. Gwenda was an actress and that was another of her wonderful performances. That

is how she would want to be remembered. The first big emotional hurdle is over.

Tony added that he did not then know whether or not the part would be re-cast but that 'we are in for many long hours of agonizing discussion.' Gwenda Wilson was replaced, by fellow Australian Betty McDowell.

Although all the preparations for Tony Shryane's retirement had been going on for months, his friends and colleagues were totally unprepared for the shock-waves that marked the end of an era. For as long as any of them had been involved and for all of its twenty-eight years, Tony *was* the programme. He nursed the writers through all their crises. He coaxed performances out of actors and actresses when the last thing they wanted to do was act. He encouraged the technicians to achieve excellence in every detail. And he charmed his secretaries with his thoughtfulness and kindness. He was somebody special to everyone and everyone lost something in his leaving.

For William Smethurst, the first day in the editor's chair must have been very difficult. In taking over from Tony Shryane, he had taken

Tony Shryane, producer for 28 years, sits in The Archers office at Pebble Mill where 7,800 scripts line the wall.

on enormous responsibilities. He was taking over what had been the BBC's most successful radio programme and he would be expected to take as much care of it as Tony had done for so long. Like many writers, he worked out his anxieties on the typewriter. The result was an exposition of his view on the future writing pattern for the programme.

I believe writers are liable to become stale and repetitive if they are required to turn out seventy-five minutes of material about the same village and the same characters indefinitely. There is also the danger that a writer on the permanent team will grow to depend entirely on The Archers for his or her livelihood. I admit to being utterly selfish, when I say I don't want to be in the position where I must either accept, month after month, bad scripts, or drop a writer whom I know depends on the programme financially. In future, I hope to establish a group of writers who can join the team for six months or a year and then drop out for a while to do other things.

I know there are dangers that the programme may suffer through lack of continuity and a confusion of style. It's important therefore that the two or three new writers needed should fit into the team and contribute something new of their own without altering the basic identity of the programme. In its mood, subject matter and season, each seventy-five minutes of material should stand and be judged in its own right, as well as forming part of a continuous saga of village life. If the characterization, narrative and quality of dialogue is any less than that of a good *Saturday Night Theatre*, then it is not good enough.

In The Archers we show the changing of the seasons and reflect the tenor of rural life. We show a pleasant world, but not an unreal world. In fact, our stories and situations must be closely researched and must be based firmly in reality. If only by virtue of being on Radio Four, we have an audience that is more intelligent and better informed than that of any other serial. We must consider this more than we have in the past, and stop 'writing-down' to our listeners. I think our listeners look to the programme as a dramatic expression of the established, rural, English way of life. They see in us the voice of the English shires.

If, at times, we seem to show a complacent, rather entrenched, middle-class society that enjoys itself, cares more about the harvest than world affairs, and refuses to agonize over the woes of the world or the terrors of the human condition, then that is what prosperous Midland villages are about. It is also what our listeners want to hear about.

Having pointed himself in the direction he wanted to go, William began to tackle what he regarded as his priority, the search for new writers. Brian Hayles's health had caused him to give up writing (he died shortly after), Keith Miles had said he wanted to concentrate on his other work, and William himself was no longer able to write scripts. The matter was urgent. He cast the net very wide, going so far as to invite applications from listeners.

Over the past two years, he has recruited a remarkable group – Alan Bower, Mary Cutler, Susan Hill, Helen Leadbeater, Tim Rose-Price and James Robson – and the writing team is now the strongest the programme has ever had. Whether or not it will produce the best results, only time will tell. What is certain is that they will be under the same scrutiny as their predecessors both from the BBC and from the listeners. Reading of the changes in the team, one woman wrote to warn them she did not expect any alteration in the course of the programme. 'The Archers has been doing very nicely and I don't want you new ones to go altering things,' she said, and then she

Helen Leadbeater, the first of the new writing team.

New writer Mary Cutler learning   Writer Alan Bower with his favour-
about the countryside.   ite ferret.

threatened: 'If you do, I shall get up a petition against the next increase in the licence fee.'

Conscious that there were plenty more like that out there, William Smethurst decided to caution the writers: 'I keep being frightened by the scripts being written at the moment. They are often very good indeed, but I live in fear and trembling lest we wake that huge, suspicious, but usually slumbering beast, Archers Public Opinion. I sometimes get scripts which appear shaped like arrows aimed at the APO's leathery hide. Once fully awakened the APO can be fierce and terrible and consume all with its flames of wrath.' The memo went on to specify The Archers' beliefs and norms, advising the writers always to balance them against the introduction of more advanced opinions. The aim was to ensure that The Archers continued to embody the kind of values so firmly held by what William called the APO.

If he ever doubts what those values are, the listeners are only too eager to tell him. After thirty years, the letters still pour in with every post, asking questions, requesting photographs, and offering advice, praise and criticism. It is a remorseless, and not always pleasant, feedback of opinions.

'I have been listening to The Archers for a very long time. To date

I find no indication of this so-called farming family actually toiling as farmers are known to do . . . instead all I get is the picture of an extremely smug, self-satisfied, indulgent clique whose only problems are the constant greed for food, riches, alcohol . . .'

'For some months now I have intended to write to you in order to express my disgust and anger at the state of The Archers. In the past six months it has progressed through weak themes, lousy casting, bad scripts, obvious actor 'loss of heart' into rubbish, and now total, undescribable drivel.'

'In many ways the new scriptwriters are excellent. They have restored to the programme the emphasis on farming and technology, country sayings and traditions. But where is the continuity? Each week is so individual it could be from an entirely different programme . . .'

'I have been moved to write to you as just lately something has happened to your programme. Today as the episode ended I had a lump in my throat and tears in my eyes . . . recently I have been laughing aloud at Jethro and Neil. The Archers are improving greatly. Keep the comedy going – and the emotion!'

'The latest scripts seem to be obsessed with highlighting class differences and preserving class barriers, and I have an awful feeling that for no other reason Shula's promising relationship with Neil is about to terminate. What an awful thought. If you're worried about the status problem can't Neil inherit a pig farm or something?'

'I wonder if you could help me. Recently an old range from Clarrie Larkin's kitchen was sold to Nelson Gabriel for his new wine bar. I missed a few relevant episodes but I would be most interested to know how much the range was sold for, as I have one that I am trying to sell myself . . .'

'Some months ago I made the suggestion that it was time The Archers produced an academic child, and suggested Lucy as a most likely candidate. I notice, to my delight, that this idea seems to be being developed. My thanks to the new writers. The Archers seems to have taken on a new lease of life – long may they continue.'

'I have been a devotee of The Archers from its very inception, and from its first broadcast The Archers has been without question the cleanest and most realistic programme ever put on the air. I was deeply shocked, however, when over the past month on three occasions swear words and blasphemy has crept in. It adds nothing to the credit of the scriptwriters, nor to the characters portrayed . . .'

If the listeners still take a keen and lively interest in the programme, so does the press, and at the beginning of 1980 stories
began to appear commenting on the writing team's most difficult
problem: the age of some characters, and the health of some older
members of cast. 'After twenty-nine years, time is catching up with
the Archers,' said the *News of the World*, and went on: 'Many of the
leading fictional characters are getting rather long in the tooth. In
real life, too, age is becoming a sad problem. To save the show the
BBC has had to develop younger characters in what was becoming
an everyday story of old folk.' An article in the *Daily Mail* listed
those members of cast in their sixties and seventies, and said:
'Ambridge, Radio Four's rural retreat, is a village with a shadow
hanging over it. The long-running agricultural soap opera has had
more than its fair share of real-life tragedy recently . . .'

Both news stories were prompted by the sudden death of Philip
Garston-Jones, who had played Jack Woolley with such warmth and
humour for seventeen years, and by the serious illness of Chris Gittins, who has played Walter Gabriel since 1953. What the newspapers
did not know was that Norman Shelley, who plays Colonel Danby,
had also been taken ill, and the writers and production staff were
going frantic re-writing, retyping scripts, and booking other actors.
In one case a set of five episodes had to be re-written twice because
of illness in the cast.

The problem does not end there. Stories can be rewritten – often
with much skill and ingenuity – but until actors are fit to record
again, the 'disappearance' of the character concerned has to be
explained. Sometimes a character can be faded into the background
and referred to by other people, and there have been classic cases in
the Archers' history of people being sent out of the village entirely
for long periods of time. Earlier this year William Smethurst and his
writers faced the problem yet again, when Gwen Berryman was
taken ill after a particularly exhausting recording session in Birmingham, and had to spend several weeks in a nursing home.

For a long time previously Gwen – severely afflicted by arthritis –
had found it difficult and tiring to travel to Pebble Mill from her
home in Torquay. She had come only for alternate recording sessions, and not at all during January and February. When she did
attend, however, her 'magic' never failed. Once at the microphone,
however ill she felt, she gave an unfaltering performance. She *was*
Doris Archer, delivering her lines with the conviction and sincerity
that has helped sustain the deep affection of listeners for thirty years.
No one listening to her on the air could guess that she had grave
difficulties in turning the pages of her script, and had to record every

Doris (Gwen Berryman) and the first Dan Archer (Harry Oakes).

Doris and the third Dan Archer, Edgar Harrison, who took over in 1969.

Doris with the second Dan Archer, Monte Crick, who took over in 1961.

scene sitting down.

For the writers, Gwen's illness meant that Doris had to be written out of the programme for the foreseeable future. For as long as possible she was simply kept 'off-stage', then Dan and Doris were sent to Guernsey to visit Lilian. In September they returned, but only Dan's voice was heard. Clumsy techniques, perhaps, but the only ones available, and Dan and Doris were, by now, very much background figures anyway.

In July, a young actor joined the programme to play the part of Dan Archer's grandson and, as evidence of his confidence for the future, William Smethurst said that the young man, David Archer, would one day take over the most famous farm in England, Brookfield, in Ambridge. But in a comment that underlines the importance of the listeners – who alone can decide whether they want to follow the fortunes of the next generation in Ambridge – the programme head said in a television interview: 'One can't say The Archers can go on and on for ever and ever. It can only go on for ever and ever if there's an audience that wants to listen.'

CHAPTER 8

The Ambridge Chronicles 1970–80

compiled by William Smethurst

1970

January saw the most astonishing event ever to happen in the village. Jennifer and Roger – now living in Borchester – received a threat that Adam would be kidnapped unless a large sum of money were paid over. Instead of telling the police, Jennifer sent Adam to stay with his grandparents at The Bull. The kidnappers – Henry Smith and Chloe Tempest – snatched him in broad daylight and carried him off to Birmingham. The police at first suspected Sid Perks, but rapidly got on the tracks of Smith and Tempest, and rescued Adam the following day.

Dan and Doris moved into Glebe Cottage, and Lilian and Nick flew to Canada, where Nick could receive specialist treatment for his eyes. Tony meanwhile sent off for details about emigrating to Australia.

Walter Gabriel was rummaging about in his shed with Dan when they found £500 in used banknotes stuffed down the back of an old armchair. PC Drury took the money away for examination, suspecting that it was part of Nelson's ill-gotten gains. Nelson at first denied all knowledge of the money, but finally told the truth: he had put it down the back of the chair as a surprise present for his father. The police returned the money.

At The Bull, Peggy wanted to close the Playbar, which was attracting a rowdy element and driving away regular customers. Jack, however, insisted that it should stay open.

On 18 March, in Canada, Nick died after falling downstairs in hospital. Lilian returned to Ambridge before the end of the month, and went back to work at the stables.

There was great activity on the Bellamy Estate, where Ralph started on a vast reorganization – reducing the ewes by half, doubling beef cattle, replacing spring barley with brussel sprouts, and doubling potatoes to two hundred acres. Tony was again threatening to go to Australia, but Bellamy made him dairy manager and sent him on a management course in Borchester instead.

After a serious fire at Manor Court, Carol and John Tregorran took shelter with Jack Woolley for several weeks. Woolley himself spent most of the summer arranging for the conversion of Arkwright Hall into a Field Study Centre.

At Brookfield, some hay was spoilt by heavy rain in late June, but after five years of excessive rain, 1970 was a comparatively good year. The corn harvest was reasonable and a mild autumn allowed ploughing to get well ahead. Dan began to regret his semi-retirement.

In the summer Sid re-formed the Ambridge cricket team, and Polly reorganized the shop on self-service lines. Walter Gabriel proposed to Mrs P (who had returned to Ambridge after the death of her second Perkins) but found he had a rival in Henry Cobb, the new cellarman at The Bull. On Mrs P's birthday, Walter gave her a budgerigar, and Henry Cobb gave her a mynah bird.

Illness struck in the autumn. Mrs P began to suffer from dizzy spells and was put on a diet, and Doris developed high blood pressure and was sent to Borchester General Hospital for tests and observation.

At Brookfield Phil and Jill got a French au pair girl called Michèle Gravencin, and Jack started to work part-time on the farm again, after complaining that Ambridge Farmers never considered him in their plans.

Bellamy asked Lilian to act as hostess at a business dinner party. He told his business friends that as a result of computer techniques he could increase his profits fourfold.

The village was astounded when Nelson Gabriel suddenly turned out to be the new owner of Hollowtree Farmhouse, which Woolley's firm had spent the summer converting into flats. Nelson offered Lilian Hollowtree Cottage at a nominal rent if she would keep an eye on the flats for him.

On 24 December, Jennifer gave birth to a baby girl, who was called Deborah.

1971

Lilian saw the New Year in with Ralph Bellamy, who tried to talk about their future together. She told him it was too soon after Nick's death, but agreed to ride his horse Red Knight at the South Borsetshire point-to-point. Nelson Gabriel returned to Ambridge rolling in money, and stayed at Grey Gables until his personal apartment at Hollowtree Flats was ready. He also saw a future with Lilian, and forced his attentions on her one night. She rejected him with scorn.

Tony Archer attended a course on 'The Spraying of Chemicals' and started going out with Roberta, Lilian's assistant at the stables.

Early in the year Jack became unwell, and had to give up his work at Brookfield. He tried to hide his illness from Peggy, but without success. Finally he went into Borchester General Hospital for tests, and was later moved to a sanatorium in Scotland.

Hugo Barnaby, John Tregorran's cousin who described himself as an international fine arts 'contact man', returned from a visit to America and bought Nightingale Farm as a rural art centre. He engaged Laura Archer as his assistant curator. In the spring, Bellamy asked him to find a suitable artist to paint a picture of Lilian on Red Knight. At the South Borsetshire point-to-point, Lilian won the Ladies Race, and Bellamy proposed to her. A week later she accepted.

At Brookfield, Gregory Salt gave in his notice and went to work as a roundsman for Borchester Dairies. Bellamy offered to help Phil with a computer assessment of his pig unit, and a 'financier' offered to buy the unit off him. Phil politely turned them both down.

At Glebe Cottage Dan had a severe attack of lumbago and Doris had trouble with decimal coinage.

There were two main talking points in early summer: a new threat to close the school, and Jack Woolley's proposal to turn a large part of his estate into a country park that would be open to visitors. The school was saved after several protest meetings, but the country park went ahead. Woolley refused to attend a discussion in the village hall and organized his own pro-Woolley meeting instead.

In July, Dan arranged for the erection of a sun lounge extension at Glebe Cottage as a surprise for Doris's birthday, and Doris was thrilled by it. Walter Gabriel bought himself some new glasses with stronger lenses, and John Tregorran bought himself an old gypsy caravan (he said it reminded him of the green caravan he lived in when he first came to Ambridge).

On 3 September, Ralph and Lilian were married. Jennifer was matron of honour, and Tony gave Lilian away. Jack was still in the sanatorium and too ill to attend the ceremony. Ralph and Lilian went to Venice for their honeymoon, and on their return moved into the Dower House.

In October, Doris gave Dan a smoking jacket for his birthday, and in November they celebrated their golden wedding anniversary.

Polly had a baby girl on 12 December, and called her Lucy.

1972

Peggy went to see Jack at the clinic in Scotland and was with him when he died on 11 January. Returning to Ambridge, she decided to move out of The Bull, and offered Sid and Polly the chance to run it. They accepted, and sold the shop to Jack Woolley. Polly became the licencee (Sid still being dogged by his criminal record).

Laura tried to buy a hundred acres of land north of Lakey Hill for a caravan park, and asked Sid to run a site shop for her. In the event

Polly Perks (Hilary Newcombe) starts work at The Bull.

the land was bought by a Welsh farmer, Haydn Evans, who planned to establish a farm for his son Gwyn.

Gregory Salt told Nora he had fallen in love with another woman, and asked for a divorce. Tony also fell in love – with a girl called Jane Petrie – and neglected his work on the Bellamy Estate. Bellamy sacked him, and he immediately went to France without telling anybody. When he returned, Phil gave him a job with Ambridge Farmers.

Woolley decided to open a steam railway at the new country park, and took Dan with him to Scotland to buy a steam engine, which he called the Empress of Ambridge. Doris was annoyed when their return was delayed, and later took to going out early in the morning without saying where she was going. She told Dan it was to teach him a lesson.

Sid and Polly moved into The Bull, and decided they could not afford two barmaids. They sacked Pru, and she told Tom he must drink somewhere else in future. Tom went through several days of suffering before she repented.

At Brookfield, Phil decided to concentrate on rearing calves for beef rather than extend the dairy herd, and bought a Friesian bull for £2,500.

In the summer, Joe Grundy, a poor tenant on Bellamy's Estate, began to intrude on village affairs. He told Peggy that two girls had spent the night with Tony at Rickyard Cottage. Tony confessed that it was true: he said the girls discussed literature all night and he fell asleep. Grundy then challenged Jethro Larkin to a tractor race and lost. He also lost out when Martha Lily, a widow from Penny Hassett whom he saw from time to time, fell in love with Joby Woodford, a forester on the Bellamy Estate.

On 20 September, an RAF trainer plane crashed near Heydon Berrow, and the entire village turned out to search for survivors. There was only the pilot on board, however, and he baled out and landed in the sewage farm at Borchester.

The following day, Dan and Tom went to check the church bells and one of the cross beams fell, hitting Dan on the shoulder. The diocesan architect confirmed that there was dry rot in the bell tower, and said the bells should not be rung in future.

Sid and Polly bought some obsolete kitchen equipment from Woolley, and opened a steak bar at The Bull. Polly helped Nora with her emotional problems when her divorce came through.

At Brookfield Jill was also suffering emotional strain. She told Phil she could not carry on any longer, and said she needed to go away somewhere alone. After the initial shock, Phil promised to arrange something. It was eventually decided that Jill should go to London and stay with an old school friend. Christine offered to cope with the children at Brookfield while she was away, and later Pru was taken on as daily help.

In November Tony had a fight with Joe Grundy and his sons, and Tom had a hoax phone call saying that Pru was in hospital in Borchester. He dashed to the hospital and poachers stole over five hundred birds from the shoot.

Martha Lily and Joby Woodford were married: the matron of honour was Mrs P, and Tom was best man.

Phil later went to London to see Jill, and they celebrated their fifteenth wedding anniversary together. Soon afterwards Jill returned home unexpectedly. She said she had fully recovered.

Martha Lily (Mollie Harris) marries Joby Woodford (George Woolley) in 1972, with Walter Gabriel (Chris Gittins) looking on.

1973

This was the year of the Ambridge Festival. Dan was elected chairman of the organizing committee, Phil agreed to run a pop group and Doris offered to look after the cottage gardens contest. Woolley underwrote the losses.

At The Bull, Sid and Polly planned a village trip to Holland for later in the year, and started catering for bed-and-breakfast visitors. Nora McAuley was appointed accommodation hostess. Not long after, Nora discovered that a new keeper on Woolley's estate – Yorkshire ex-policeman George Barford – was an alcoholic. She tried to befriend him, but he was unwilling to be helped. He told her his wife was a Catholic, and there could be no future for them.

Bellamy took over as chairman of Ambridge Wanderers football team, and told Sid (the manager) that he expected more team discipline in future. Phil became leader of Ambridge Scout Troop, and Woolley gave him a bugle.

On 30 March, Lilian gave birth to a son, James Rodney Dominic. She engaged a nanny called Mrs Beard. Woolley sold Ambridge Hall to Laura, then found she had not enough money to buy it. (Disastrous dealings on the stock exchange also forced her to sack Fairlie and sell her motor car.) Woolley worked out a scheme by which Laura could occupy the Hall during her lifetime, after which it would revert to him.

In May, there was a robbery at Grey Gables. Peggy found Woolley seriously injured in the club lounge, and he was rushed to hospital. He did not regain consciousness for several days. Paintings and silver were stolen.

Both Doris and Jill worried about Phil suffering from overwork and strain, particularly after he crashed his car on the way home from Borchester. A breathalyzer test proved negative.

It was a difficult year with the livestock at Brookfield. Horace the bull was found to be infertile and had to be sold for beef; a bull calf called Jolly died from lead poisoning; and a ewe aborted after being worried by a dog. In June, thirty ewes and their lambs were stolen from Lakey Hill.

A 'new entrant' apprentice, Neil Carter from Birmingham, joined Ambridge Farmers and accidentally mowed a field of oats. Elizabeth was rushed to hospital after eating mercury-dressed grain.

In June, Jill heard that the village school was finally to close, and there was no chance of a reprieve. Woolley threatened to close the village shop, but changed his mind after Walter and Mrs P presented him with a petition from the Over-Sixties. He took on Martha

Woodford as sub-postmistress, and she took in Neil Carter as a lodger.

The Ambridge Festival was a success, and Phil organized singing by the Ambridge Folk Chorale. Doris held a wine and cheese party for those connected with the cottage gardens contest.

In August, Woolley was told by Valerie that she wanted a divorce, and immediately collapsed with a heart attack. He was ordered to rest, and Peggy took over running Grey Gables.

Many villagers, including Dan, Doris, Carol Tregorran, and Christine, went on Sid's trip to Holland. A good time was had by all.

Tony left Ambridge Farmers, and went into partnership with Haydn Evans at Willow Farm. Soon afterwards he met a travelling farm secretary, Mary Weston, and fell in love with her.

It was a difficult autumn for Joe Grundy. After spending some weeks in hospital with farmers' lung he was put on a strict diet by his doctor, and collapsed from malnutrition outside The Bull. When he recovered he crashed his lorry into the village pump and demolished it.

At The Bull, Sid and Polly closed the steak bar and planned to reopen it as the Ploughman's Bar, serving home-made food.

At Christmas, Ambridge's old roadman Zebedee Tring was discovered dead in his cottage, his dog Gyp and cat Queenie beside him. They were both found good homes.

1974

Early in the year, Laura organized WI members to bake pastries and pies for the new Ploughman's Bar at The Bull, and Tony and Mary Weston held their engagement party there on 24 January. But Tony was having a difficult first winter at Willow Farm. The soaring cost of feedstuffs led him to rely too heavily on silage, and his milk yields fell. The dairy complained about low butter-fat content in his milk, and two cows were blown through eating clover. Then four heifers developed New Forest disease. By June – with calves fetching only £1 each at Borchester Market – he was only just keeping his head above water, and was relieved he had not gone in for pigs or beef cattle.

Paul Johnson flew off to work in Germany, and Roger Travers-Macy took a job away from home, selling antiquarian books.

Tom and Pru found George Barford semi-conscious in the Lodge: he had attempted suicide by taking sleeping pills. When Nora McAuley found out, she moved into the Lodge with him, and said she intended to stay. George did not object, but many villagers were scandalized. George rose in popular esteem, however, when he spotted strangers loitering round the Dower House, and with help from Tom and Harry Booker caught thieves robbing the house with a removal van.

In March, there was an outbreak of SVD at Hollowtree and Phil's entire herd was slaughtered. He later replaced them with minimal-disease pigs. Dan had several ewe hogs stolen from Lakey Hill, and Phil started freeze-branding his cows to deter cattle rustlers.

Neil Carter met a girl called Sandy Miller, and went with her to a wild party in Borchester. The party was raided by the police, and drugged cigarettes were found in Neil's pocket. He was placed on probation by Borchester magistrates.

Ann Moore watched Shula riding Mister Jones and said she showed promise as a competition rider. Phil agreed to support her, if she would also do a secretarial course at Borchester Tech.

In competition with Walter, Joe Grundy opened a caravan site, and Walter maliciously sent some tinkers to stay on it. Joe sent them back

Lilian (Elizabeth Marlow) on the left, and right, Shula (Judy Bennett) meet showjumper Ann Moore.

to Walter's caravan site, and Walter got PC Drury to move them out of the village altogether.

In the summer, Tony received a letter from Mary Weston breaking off their engagement, and Jennifer said she wanted a separation from Roger. She moved into Wynford's with Christine, and started going out bowling with Woolley's second keeper, Gordon Armstrong. Their late return from Borchester caused comment in the village.

Jack Woolley proposed to Peggy and she refused him. She became friendly with a man called Dave Escott who was starting an interior design business, but later discovered he was just touting for business.

It was a good harvest at Willow Farm, and Tony sold his corn straight off the combine. He met Haydn Evans's niece, Pat Lewis, who had come to help her uncle after he slipped a disc. Not long after, Pat proposed to him and he accepted.

In November, Bellamy was told by a Harley Street specialist that he needed complete rest if he were to avoid a heart attack. He decided to retire: he and Lilian would sell the estate and leave the village, keeping only one thousand acres as a future inheritance for James.

Polly was found to have an ectopic pregnancy in a Fallopian tube, and went into hospital for an operation.

At Brookfield, Kenton left to go to sea as a merchant navy cadet, and Shula became friendly with a much older man – hi-fi fanatic Eric Selwyn – at Borchester Tech.

John Tregorran went on a lecture tour of America after warning Hugo Barnaby to stay clear of Carol.

Towards the end of the year Pat and Tony were married.

1975

The year got off to an exciting start when bandits set up a road block and tried to attack the post-bus – carrying Walter and Laura – with iron bars. Harry Booker drove the bus over the fields to safety, and Laura cracked her false teeth.

Dan shot Joe Grundy's dog, Jacko, when he saw it apparently worrying sheep. He later bought Joe another dog.

After a row with George, Nora moved back to The Bull and told Polly she was pregnant. Shortly afterwards she had a miscarriage, and George asked her to move back to the Lodge and make a fresh start.

At Willow Farm, Pat bought one hundred free-range hens, and Tony exchanged his sports car for a van.

The break-up of the Bellamy Estate brought a newcomer to the village: rich, thirty-two-year-old bachelor Brian Aldridge, who

Tony (Colin Skipp) and Pat (Patricia Gallimore) soon after they were married.

bought 1500 acres and a farmhouse. Carol Tregorran gave a dinner party for him, and he met Jennifer (who had now been asked for a divorce by Roger). He started taking her out to dinner now and then.

After an outbreak of vandalism, PC Drury suspected Neil of wrecking phone boxes and spraying the Pounds' farm-shop sign with paint. He searched Neil's locker at Brookfield – without permission – and was attacked by a furious Jill, who threatened to complain to the chief constable. Drury apologized.

At Hollowtree two pigs died from fighting, and others developed anaemia when Neil forgot to give them iron injections. On Lakey Hill, Dan's sheep developed twin-lambing disease when he cut back the feed to his in-lamb ewes.

Despite the village's misgivings, Joe Grundy held a successful pop concert at Grange Farm.

In the early summer, John Tregorran returned home from America and said he was back for good. Kenton returned too, on leave, and brought Shula a grass skirt from Tahiti. Paul Johnson came back to Ambridge only briefly. After an extraordinary series of jobs (including flying helicopters and opening German exhibition sites), he had ended up as an engineer on a Welsh oil rig. No oil had been found, and he now had a new job in London.

Polly's father, arsonist Frank Mead, died in a mental hospital. After a long search, Sid and Polly bought a cottage in Penny Hassett for £4,500 and started to renovate it. Sid voted 'no' in the Common Market referendum.

The summer was hot and dry – hardly any rain fell during June, July and August – and at Home Farm Brian Aldridge found his spring barley hardly worth harvesting, and his sugar beet yields far lower than he had expected. At Brookfield, however, Phil was delighted by his maize, which withstood the drought and grew quickly with the first September rains.

Joe Grundy won first prize with his marrows at the Flower and Produce Show, and also won first prize in Laura's raffle in aid of church funds: the prize was a luxury weekend for two at Grey Gables.

Work on the re-hanging of the church bells began, and the vicar moved into a new vicarage. Walter took a bottle of elderberry wine to the housewarming party, and made Doris tiddly.

More seriously, Jethro broke his leg when he fell through the floor of a loft at Brookfield. Phil was almost prosecuted for negligence – the floor was unsafe – and had to pay Jethro compensation.

In October Laura roused the Ambridge Protection Society to stop the last surviving elm tree in the village from being cut down, and Jack Woolley accepted a race horse – Grey Silk – in settlement of a debt.

Doris and Christine were Christmas shopping when they met Carol in a Felpersham store. A store detective accused Carol of shoplifting, and two pens – unpaid for – were found in her bag. The shop said they would prosecute.

On 31 December, Pat gave birth to a son, John Daniel.

1976

The year started well for Brian Aldridge when he proposed to Jennifer and she accepted, and for Carol Tregorran who was found not guilty of shoplifting at Felpersham Crown Court. (She had dropped the pens in to her bag accidentally while chatting to Doris and Christine.)

Joe Grundy arrived alone at Grey Gables for his luxury weekend for two, and annoyed Woolley by demanding the other half of his prize in cash. Woolley was further irritated to find that Higgs was using the Bentley to visit his lady friend at Hollerton Junction.

Tom retired as sporting manager at Grey Gables (Woolley gave him a silver tea service) and started work at Woolley's new garden centre, which opened at Easter.

Jennifer's divorce came through, and she and Brian were married quietly at Borchester Registry Office. Brian bought her twelve Jacob sheep, and she took up spinning and weaving.

A new editor for the *Borchester Echo* was taken on by Jack Woolley, a young man called Simon Parker, formerly a reporter on the *Felpersham Evening Post*. Another new face was Laura's lodger, Colonel Frederick Danby, who had retired from the army and worked as regional organizer for a national charity.

At Brookfield, Shula made friends with Michele Brown, a New Zealand girl who came to Ambridge with a shearing gang. They arranged to go for a holiday hitch-hiking round Europe together. But matters were overshadowed by Jill's illness. After complaining about tiredness for several weeks, she collapsed and was rushed to Borchester General Hospital suffering from a thyroid deficiency. She was in hospital for three weeks.

In July, at the village fête, George Barford played a cornet solo with the Hollerton Town Band, and Christine organized a pony club display. Paul arrived home unexpectedly and confessed that he had been having an affair with another woman, but it was all over. All he wanted was to return to Christine and Peter. He resigned his London job, but the other woman – called Brenda – followed him to Ambridge. Christine sent her packing.

At Brookfield, Phil took on another farm worker, Fred Wakefield, and at the market garden Carol lost her manager, Arthur Tovey, who died when his aluminium ladder touched a power cable.

After Michele Brown returned from holiday with Shula, she took a job at Grey Gables as a waitress and moved into Nightingale Farm with Neil. But Neil's affections were all for Shula. He fell in love with her and his work began to suffer. Shula, however, was more interested in Simon Parker, the new editor of the *Echo*, and in the campaign to stop Borchester Grammar School from going comprehensive. She helped organize a 'Save Borchester Grammar' protest march, to Jill's considerable annoyance.

In November, Laura organized an Edwardian Evening at Grey Gables, and at Stow Fair Brian bought Debbie a skewbald pony called Moonbeam. Home Farm was burgled by youths, and a radio and £50 were stolen.

Dan and Doris went to Guernsey to visit Lilian, and Doris caught bronchitis. They were both away from Ambridge for Christmas.

1977

At the beginning of the year, Dan was made chairman of the committee organizing celebrations for the Queen's Jubilee, to take place in June.

George's son, Terry Barford (who had come to Ambridge after getting into trouble with the police), was patrolling the woods with his father when he came across Joe Grundy, and hit him over the head. It turned out, however, that Grundy was not poaching, but earth-stopping for the hunt. Then in April, Terry got into more trouble, when he was arrested after being found drunk in possession of a stolen car, which he had driven into a lamp-post. He was later sent to a detention centre for three months.

Part of Walter Gabriel's cottage roof blew off in a storm and Doris persuaded him to stay at Glebe Cottage for a while. In the following weeks he moved on to Brookfield, Wynford's, and Mary Pound's house.

Shula organized a children's meet for the hunt, and Jennifer took Adam and Debbie hunting for the first time. But Phil was depressed

Dominoes in The Bull. Left to right, Tony (Colin Skipp), Walter Gabriel (Chris Gittins), Tom Forrest (Bob Arnold) and Dan (Edgar Harrison), watched by Sid Perks (Alan Devereux) and Nora (Julia Mark).

that Shula had begun to go out regularly with Simon Parker, whom he referred to as 'that inky blighter'. Nor was he pleased to hear that Jill had joined an action group to stop Borchester Grammar going independent. Both he and Shula accused her of mixing with some very odd left-wing types.

Jethro developed gum trouble, and started leaving his denture in unexpected places. Jill forcibly took him to the dentist, who extracted his last remaining teeth.

The 'Supercooks' scheme was begun by Shula and Michele, catering for peoples' private dinner parties. Then, after Shula danced with Alf Grundy at a Young Conservative hop, Joe gave her a French cookery book that had belonged to his wife Susan. He told Jill that he would welcome Shula as a daughter-in-law. Later this year, Shula rode Mister Jones in the South Borsetshire point-to-point and came fourth. But she finally abandoned hopes of a career with horses, and got a job with Rodway and Watson, a small Borchester estate agent.

The garden at Nightingale Farm was devastated when Grundy's two pigs escaped and ran amok. Michele impounded the pigs until Grundy paid her £25 compensation.

In May, Pat's mother was taken ill in Wales, and she went to look after her. Tony started flirting with the district milk-recording girl, Libby Jones, and scandalized the rest of the Archer family by taking her to the Cricket Club dance. Jennifer thought he was having an affair, but Brian doubted he was capable.

The following month Dan slipped and strained his back while watching the lighting of the Jubilee bonfire on Lakey Hill. Shula and Neil stayed on Lakey Hill until early morning, watching the string of bonfires as far away as Malvern and Wenlock Edge. Dan did manage to attend the Jubilee party and barbecue, but in a wheelchair.

Paul Johnson started a fish farm and sold the paddock at Wynford's to pay for it, and Tony was offered the tenancy of Bridge Farm by his brother-in-law Ralph. Mike Tucker approached Haydn Evans about taking over Tony's partnership, and Haydn agreed to the idea.

While out riding with his girl-friend, Sarah Brinkley, Adam was bitten by an adder and taken to Borchester General Hospital. He was seriously ill, and only recovered after being treated with a new type of vaccine.

Neil meanwhile had recruited Shula to help run the youth club, and she recruited him for the Young Conservatives.

At The Bull, Sid took on a temporary barmaid, Caroline Bone from Darrington, who had finished a cordon bleu cookery course in London and wanted to prove to her mother that she could earn her own keep.

On 30 September, Jennifer gave birth to a daughter, Katherine Victoria.

At the fish-farm, twenty thousand seven-inch trout were lost when a filter was blocked. Paul went bankrupt and then disappeared in Christine's car. It was found next day in London. Eventually Paul was discovered in Hamburg: he told Christine he was never coming back.

The Tuckers were forced to leave Rickyard Cottage (Phil needed it for his new cowman, Graham Collard) and moved into Willow Farm with Pat and Tony. To Pat's horror, Mike turned out to be a Country and Western addict, and brought his record player with him.

1978

An eventful year for Christine began when she moved out of Wynford's and into the stables' farmhouse (now owned by Ambridge Farmers). George Barford helped chop wood for her and they became friends. She was able to sympathize from personal experience when Nora left George and went to live with a man in Borchester. Soon after, word came that Paul had been killed in a car crash in Germany.

Jethro astounded the village by announcing that his Uncle Charlie had died and left him a fortune. Clarrie gave up her cleaning jobs and became a lady of leisure before discovering that the fortune amounted to only £4,200. Clarrie went back to cleaning, and Jethro bought a second-hand car with Neil.

In February, Tony and Pat moved into Bridge Farm and bought themselves a second-hand herringbone milking parlour.

At The Bull, Sid took on a new barmaid – Jackie Smith, a Londoner who had come to Borchester in pursuit of a brewery rep.

In March, Shula and Mary Pound found Joe Grundy delirious in his farmhouse, suffering from a bad dose of flu, and abandoned by Eddie and his girlfriend. Joe's cows were infected with brucellosis, and his favourite hob ferret, Turk, was discovered dead in a trap. Joe said he was past caring about anything.

At Home Farm, Brian hit a work-shy employee, Jack Roberts, after giving him the sack. When Mike Tucker took up the man's case, Jennifer threw a garden rake at him. Peggy said Jennifer had become more violent since she had met Brian.

Ambridge celebrated May Day in the traditional English manner, with Maypole dancing and a May Queen. During the festivities Simon Parker told Shula he was leaving the *Borchester Echo* and going to work in London.

Jennifer and Brian – irritated by delays over the building of their swimming pool – went on holiday to the Seychelles. When they came back, Jennifer decided to get an au pair girl. A few weeks later Eva Lenz (a blonde nineteen-year-old from Stuttgart) arrived at Home Farm.

David Archer once again failed his A-level maths, and had to give up his plans to go to university. Instead he decided to take a two year course at agricultural college.

In July Neil was rushed to hospital suffering from Weil's disease, which he had picked up from touching rat's urine with a cut hand. He was ill for some weeks, then went to a union convalescent home. When he returned, Mike Tucker blackmailed him into taking on the job of local union secretary.

The following month, Doris was upset when Woolley announced a scheme to build houses opposite Glebe Cottage. The parish council opposed the development but Woolley called a parish meeting and gained widespread support. The scheme – Glebelands – went ahead.

Jill was persuaded to join Jennifer in a craft shop venture at Home Farm called the Two Jays. But when Walter realized his carved wooden animals were a success in the shop, he took them away and opened his own Wally G craft studio. Both ventures ended in disaster. Jill was £150 in debt, and Phil had to find the money.

In the autumn, things improved for Joe Grundy, when Eddie returned to Grange Farm and the two of them started a turkey venture. Joe's cows were slaughtered under the brucellosis eradication scheme, and he received full compensation.

Life began to look brighter for George Barford as well. His divorce came through, and Terry wrote to say he had joined the army – the Prince of Wales Own Regiment of Yorkshire. George asked Christine to marry him, and she said yes. She also said she wanted to be married in church, and after much heartsearching, Richard Adamson agreed to perform the ceremony.

1979

The year began badly for Brian Aldridge when, in January, a hungry vixen took several of his early lambs and proved too cunning for the hunt. In the end, Brian went out and shot it – then was too ashamed to tell anyone.

At The Bull, Jackie left in pursuit of a sports instructor called Basil, and Caroline Bone returned after the collapse of her Bristol wine bar. Sid offered her the chance to prepare exciting food for the Ploughman's.

Martha Woodford developed mild pneumonia, and was off work for several weeks. When she returned, she told Woolley she could not cope by herself, so Woolley decided to sell the shop, and told Martha the new buyer would probably give her the sack. Carol Tregorran and Peggy tried to form a syndicate with Martha to take the shop over, but Woolley dismissed their offer as ludicrous. In the end, he decided to keep the shop, and hired Dorothy Adamson to help Martha two afternoons a week.

On 1 March, Christine and George were married in Ambridge parish church. Tom was best man, and Christine wore a wedding dress of cream and old-gold satin.

Phil decided to bid for thirty acres of Meadow Farm, and Brian agreed to buy Hollowtree pig unit as the basis of a large-scale pig-fattening venture. When half the village objected, he gave the idea up, and left Phil struggling for cash to buy his land.

On 16 April, Pat gave birth to a daughter, Helen, who had a dislocated hip and had to wear a special harness for three months.

There was ill health in the village this spring. Doris suffered from mouth ulcers under her dental plate, and Sid collapsed with an ear infection immediately after sending Polly and Lucy to Weston for a holiday. Walter Gabriel developed a more serious complaint, and was taken to hospital suffering from a sugar inbalance. All attempts to track down Nelson failed – his London office was discovered to be a seedy accommodation address in Notting Hill.

Carol Tregorran nearly bought a second-hand Jaguar off Harry Booker, then discovered it was a 'ringer' – the front of one car and the back of another, joined in the middle.

At Grange Farm, Joe Grundy was delighted when Eddie proposed to marry Dolly Treadgold. He put up new curtains in the parlour and looked forward to welcoming his daughter-in-law and unpaid housekeeper. Eddie and Dolly soon split up, however, and Sinclair gave Joe six months to improve the farm or face eviction.

In early summer, Shula decided to go on an overland trip across Asia, then on to visit Michele Brown in New Zealand. Phil reluctantly agreed to find the money and Shula set off – accompanied by Nick Wearing, who had spent several months at Brookfield gaining practical farming experience.

Grundy went to the Royal Show in early July, and was impressed by a display of deer farming and the possibility of selling deer's velvet to the Japanese as an aphrodisiac. Jennifer entered one of her Jacobs, but failed to win anything.

At Bridge Farm, Tony was confused when Pat went off to Wales with the children, saying she did not want him to go with her. He

Shula Archer (Judy Bennett).

spent two anxious weeks worrying about his marriage before Pat returned home. She made him promise to relax more and work less.

Eddie and Dolly Treadgold got engaged again, and Joe prepared the turkey shed for a lavish reception. He borrowed the Brookfield flags, and ordered vast quantities of chicken legs and vol-au-vents from Caroline. The day before the wedding, however, Eddie called it off – he said Dolly was too flighty.

Nelson Gabriel turned up unexpectedly, saying he had been in Venezuela and Spain. He took Walter abroad for a holiday.

Shula phoned from Bangkok to say all her money had been stolen. Phil had to telex funds to her, and she arrived home with a prayer wheel for Jill. She asked Phil to pay her hunt subscription.

Caroline Bone went to work at Grey Gables, and Nelson stayed there after bringing Walter home from Tenerife. Nelson bounced a cheque at The Bull, and Woolley discovered he was penniless and kicked him out. He spent a miserable Christmas with Walter at Honeysuckle Cottage.

Ambridge's new policeman, PC Coverdale, proposed to Eva and was accepted.

1980

At Brookfield, Phil planned a major reorganization of the farm – increasing the sheep to three hundred ewes, draining the new thirty acres, and applying for a potato quota. He failed to get an FHDS grant (designed for inefficient farmers) and sold his beef cattle to Brian Aldridge.

Nelson continued to run up debts. Woolley finally paid them off on condition he left the area. Nelson went – only to return a few weeks later and repay every penny he owed. To Walter's delight, he stayed in Borchester and opened a wine bar.

In Guernsey, Ralph Bellamy died after a heart attack. Lilian returned to Ambridge and annoyed Tony by refusing to discuss his need for a silage clamp. She scandalized Peggy by drinking and being friendly with Eddie Grundy. Eddie captained The Cat and Fiddle darts team when they beat The Bull team in a 'friendly' match, and Lilian gave the victors a brass Viking.

John Tregorran and Jennifer organized a study group to carry out a landscape survey of Ambridge. Colonel Danby, Pat and Caroline agreed to help.

Pat and Tony decided to go into pigs in a small way, and bought two in-pig sows from Phil. Colonel Danby also bought a pig, and called it Edric.

Mrs P was scandalized by Eva's nocturnal visits to the police house. When her purse was lost in Borchester she told the desk sergeant about PC Coverdale's immorality, and Coverdale was severely rebuked.

At Grange Farm, Joe Grundy went back into milk, and built up a herd of twenty cows. Eddie got a job as a lorry driver, but gave it up when Joe finally agreed to pay him a wage. Eddie also started walking out with Clarrie Larkin, but Jethro was horrified and said she would come to ruin.

On 9 May, Eva was married to PC Coverdale in Ambridge parish church. She wore a cream silk, full-length, Empire line wedding dress, the reception was at Home Farm, and they went on honeymoon to the Canaries.

Jennifer was just about the last person in the village to realize that John Tregorran had fallen in love with her. He made his feelings clear during a survey of Leaders Wood, and Jennifer fled from him.

John immediately went to America to organize a series of antique fairs.

Shula found a new boyfriend: Mark Hebden, a twenty-six-year-old solicitor. She soon decided he was boring, but he recovered ground with her after running to the rescue of a fallow deer being attacked by a lurcher in the country park. The deer kicked him, Shula helped him to Grey Gables, and Caroline put him to bed.

Tony got tetanus poisoning and was seriously ill for several weeks. Soon after he recovered, Pat discovered that she was pregnant again.

Spray drift from one of Brian's fields badly affected Carol's market garden crops.

In July, David returned home from college and joined his father at Brookfield. After some initial tension he settled down happily and helped Phil to set up the new sheep handling yards and to buy three hundred ewes for Lakey Hill. He alarmed Jill by going out with the notorious playgirl Jackie Woodstock, Shula's arch-rival on the committee of Borchester Young Conservatives. David's twenty-first birthday was celebrated in style with a dance in the barn at Brookfield. Four days later the family remembered a less happy anniversary for Phil: on 22 September it was twenty-five years since the death of Grace in the stables at Grey Gables.

Colonel Danby wrestled with his conscience and finally proposed to Laura, but she turned him down. The Over Sixties Club turned down Laura's plan for the traditional outing to Weston, and went on a jaunt to London organized by Nelson Gabriel.

The Coverdales' marriage became a talking point when Eva turned up on the doorstep at Home Farm in tears, and Coverdale refused to collect her for several days. They resolved their differences, however, and departed happily to Plymouth, where Jim felt his promotion prospects would be better.

Lizzie Larkin died. Jethro was badly affected and slow to recover from the shock. Clarrie reluctantly stopped seeing Eddie Grundy for a while.

Dan and Doris spent several weeks of the summer with Lilian in Guernsey.

Jennifer's parish survey team made the major discovery of a forgotten medieval village, and were horrified to find evidence that an ancient stone chapel was now part of the Grundys' cider cellar.

CHAPTER 9

Fitting in the Farming

by Anthony Parkin,
Agricultural Story Editor

'Are you the chap that does the farming for The Archers?' I had just picked up the telephone in my office at Pebble Mill.

'Yes,' I admitted, guardedly, since the speaker sounded a little irritated.

'Well, let me tell you that you don't know a flaming thing about it,' my anonymous caller went on.

'Hang on a mo—' I started, but it was no good. Out it all came.

'Look, you've got Phil Archer drilling barley this week. Well, let me tell you that I've got six chaps out in one of my sheds playing cards. It's so wet no one's drilling barley this week – not even in Ambridge. I tell you, you just don't know a flaming thing about it!'

'Well, let me—' I began again, but I was wasting my time. He had slammed the phone down. Doubtless he felt a lot better for giving that bloke on The Archers an earful, since there's nothing so frustrating as waiting to get on with the drilling in a late spring, especially when you are paying half a dozen men to do nothing.

What he did not know, and what I was trying to tell him, and what he may never know unless he chances to read this book, is that the episode which had offended him when it was broadcast in the second week of April had been written at the beginning of January when the snow lay on the ground.

This is one of the eternal headaches of having to prepare the scripts so far in advance when dealing with a seasonal subject like farming. If Phil Archer were producing nuts and bolts instead of pigs and cows everything would be much easier, since he could carry on equally well in January as July. But you cannot drill spring barley all the year round. It has been sown as early as February and as late as May, and is usually put in between mid-March and mid-April in the Ambridge area. The second week of April ought to have been 'safe'. It just happened to be raining hard all week – and the week before and the week before that. Hence our friend's agitation.

Most of the time we manage to avoid trouble, largely by not sticking our necks out. We did come unstuck in the drought year of 1976 when we had a crisis during harvest caused by a breakdown in the corn drier at Brookfield, a perfectly reasonable event in a normal year. The trouble was that 1976 was far from normal. We had virtually no rain for three or four months, harvest in the Ambridge area was over by early August and almost no corn drying was done anywhere. So our drama over the drier in mid-August sounded totally unreal.

I think the period when I did most nail-biting was when we decided to have an outbreak of SVD at Brookfield. SVD, or swine vesicular disease to give it its proper name, cropped up for the first time suddenly and devastatingly in December 1972. It rampaged through the country causing the compulsory slaughter of hundreds of thousands of pigs. It was an obvious subject for inclusion in The Archers but the trouble was that no one knew how long it would last. Every time the Ministry of Agriculture vets announced that they thought it was under control, it broke out again. And I kept wishing that we had, after all, decided to give Phil's farm a dose of the disease.

Eventually we came to a point in November 1973 when we decided to take the plunge. The Ministry vets wanted us to deal with SVD because it could be used to put across a lot of points they needed to get over to farmers, farm workers, hauliers, dealers and others. It obviously had great dramatic potential, with Phil Archer's pigs being wiped out. The question was, would a disease which we were dis-cussing at script conference in November still be around by March when the resulting scripts were broadcast? No one knew, not even the Ministry. Suppose it were all over in January or February and we were stuck with an outbreak in Ambridge in March – not an odd scene which could be scrapped without difficulty nearer the time but a story running through the scripts for several weeks? I outlined my predicament to the Ministry vets and managed to extract a promise from them that, whatever happened, they would not announce the eradication of SVD until after the Hollowtree outbreak. On that basis, we went ahead. I must have been the only person in the country praying for the odd outbreak in January and February 1974. We got the necessary trickle of cases and then the Ambridge flare-up. I need not have worried. Unhappily the disease is still with us in 1980.

So, unfortunately, is the gap between the planning and the broad-casting of The Archers, which is why you never hear anyone being too precise. You do not hear Phil Archer boasting to Brian Aldridge that he got two ton of barley to the acre, because our writers are dealing with combining the crop when the real Phil Archers of this world are still drilling theirs. So, when he is asked how his corn has yielded, Phil replies rather blandly: 'Not as well as I'd hoped for,' or, 'Better than I'd expected.' These are phrases to which the real farmer can relate in the light of the real harvest, and I am not left with egg on my face as a result of Brookfield harvesting three ton of wheat in a season when most people only managed thirty hundredweight.

By and large I think we manage fairly well, as I am often approached by people who want something topical 'put over' in The Archers, and who obviously have no idea from listening to the pro-gramme that it is prepared so far in advance. Indeed one senior official of the Ministry of Agriculture's advisory service refused point blank recently to believe it. 'It can't have been written three months ago,' he declared, 'it's too accurate.' I think he felt I was simply making an excuse for not being able to do anything about his request.

Not that we do go in for 'putting over' Ministry or indeed any other organization's propaganda, although no one can deny that the programme has had a strong 'educational' influence over the years. This was more true in the earlier days than it is now, when any benefits of this kind come as a bonus rather than as one of the pro-gramme's prime objectives. There are good reasons for the changing emphasis. The Archers was, after all, born as a result of a suggestion made by a farmer at an agricultural meeting called by the BBC to discuss how it could serve farmers better. The serial was launched while food was still rationed (the meat ration had just been reduced to 10d – that's 4p worth per person per week) and when farming's great technological revolution was just getting under way. There was plenty of advice to put over, and radio, especially radio drama, was one of the most effective ways of getting the message across. So when Dan and Phil took it in turns solemnly to go through a Min-istry leaflet on warble fly control, almost paragraph by paragraph, it was not only justified but perfectly acceptable to the listeners who either wanted to know about the life cycle of the warble fly or, if they did not, were happy that someone else upon whom they were depending for their food did.

Nowadays, as a responsible farmer, Phil still dresses his cattle against warble fly – Dan is getting a bit too old to play an active part, though he still looks on – but this activity is probably used only as a background for a discussion with Tom Forrest or Colonel Danby or whoever else happens to be passing (people are forever passing in The Archers) about a road-widening scheme or the church roof or Eddie Grundy's latest escapade. My job is to make sure that Phil is dressing his cattle at the right time of year and that anything which is said on the subject is accurate and apposite. If any farmer listening thinks, 'Oh Heavens, I haven't done mine yet,' and rushes out and treats his animals – well that is a bonus.

Farming in this country has seen more changes since The Archers started than in any thirty years since the dawn of time – a pretty sweeping statement, you may think, but impossible to contradict. If the fictional Dan Archer had settled down to look at the real *Farmers Weekly* on that first Friday of that first week in January 1951, he would have been able to read a review of farming during the first half of the twentieth century. Running to eleven pages, it was a remark-able story of achievement and yet I doubt if even the precocious Phil, had he been looking over his father's shoulder, could have foreseen the developments of the next thirty years.

It is true that the revolution was under way and that some of its course had been charted, but no one at that time could have predicted the speed or the extent of its passage. Not even Phil, as he harnessed up Blossom and Boxer the following morning and looked forward to replacing them soon with a neat little grey tractor with a mounted plough, not even he could have foreseen that in his father's lifetime he would be having his land drained by a machine costing £100,000 and using a laser beam to keep it level.

This is not the place to detail the transformation which has taken place in our agriculture since The Archers took to the air, although most of it has been reflected at one time or another in Ambridge farming. If an observant traveller were to return to the village after a thirty-year absence, what would he note, apart from the absence of elms killed by Dutch elm disease a few years back? He would see a more open countryside with bigger fields resulting from the removal of hedges, although nothing like as dramatic in Ambridge as in the predominantly arable areas of the country. He would see the fields full of black and white Friesian cattle instead of the reds and roans of the Shorthorns he had left behind in 1951. He would see fewer men working in the fields – and he would not see much of them, as they would be inside the now compulsory tractor cabs, probably listening to Radio One. He would notice, perhaps, the absence of hay and corn ricks and that there were no milk churns at the ends of the lanes

– the bulk tanker reigns supreme these days. He would see that the hedges were neatly trimmed rather than laid, and that the corn fields were free of weeds. He would notice new, large farm buildings and possibly the odd tower silo, but the picture, apart from being to a perceptive visitor slightly different, would not be a displeasing one. He probably would not realize that Pettifer's barn had gone, for example, although its removal caused such a commotion at the time; in fact many of Ambridge's own residents have no doubt forgotten that it ever existed.

The two main trends as Phil moved from youth to middle age have been a growth in size of everything – farms, fields, herds, flocks, machines – and a move towards specialization. Apart from Tony's recent dabbling in pigs in a small way (in part a reaction against too much specialization), he is a dairy farmer pure and simple, growing a few acres of barley only until he gets his herd up to its maximum. When Mr Elliott was tenant of Bridge Farm in 1951 he had a much smaller dairy herd but also a flock of sheep, a small pig herd, hens, ducks, geese, and grew oats and barley to feed his stock as well as kale for the cows and turnips for the sheep.

Here are a few figures to illustrate the trends which have taken place over the Archer years. They are very approximate, due to changes in methods of classifying data and availability of up-to-date information.

	Then	*Now*
Farms	380,000	190,000
Average farm size	63 acres	126 acres
Full time workers	553,000	160,000
Combines	16,000	48,000
Working horses	261,000	virtually none
Dairy herds	144,000	43,000
Milk/cow/year	754 gallons	1,050 gallons
Eggs/hen/year	150	250
Wheat/acre	22 cwt	40 cwt
Poultry meat produced	100,000 tons	675,000 tons
Milk produced	1,530m gallons	2,800m gallons
Fertilizer (nutrients)	850,000 tons	2,000,000 tons

All of this has been made possible by the enormous strides made by agricultural scientists, by machinery designers and manufacturers, plant breeders, drug companies, chemical firms and many others whose work would no doubt be derided by Jethro Larkin – who, at the same time, finds life much easier as a result of all their efforts.

But although life may be easier to the extent that a farm worker does not spend all day now walking behind a plough or slashing a hedge, it is amazing how similar Phil's daily routine is in 1980 to Dan's thirty years ago. He still gets up early and is on the go dealing with the expected and the unexpected all day. Though, to be fair, there is more pressing of buttons and pulling levers rather than humping sacks and forking muck, and instead of mowing thistles he is more likely to be supervising the mixing of a 'cocktail' of chemical sprays measured to the nearest millilitre which will make sure that not only the thistles but any other unwanted plant is killed.

And yet, reassuringly, nature and the seasons still hold sway. Phil still has to milk his cows twice a day, including Sundays, and he still cannot turn them out if it is too wet or it has not been warm enough to make the grass grow. New diseases threaten all the time, ready to attack his crops and stock, and if a ewe gives birth without any milk the lambs still have to be fostered or fed from a bottle. Drains still get blocked and gates come off their hinges. Livestock still get out and do damage and if Blossom's foot is no longer likely to hold up field work, a puncture in the tractor tyre will.

Some time ago I was asked by the script writers for a guide to a typical day for Ambridge's main farmers. Here was Phil's:

6.00	Gets up.
6.10	Listens to Farming Today while he shaves and dresses.
6.30	Makes a cup of tea and takes one to Jill.
6.40	Goes out. Calls in at dairy to see Graham Collard. Drives and walks round farm and buildings deciding what to do that day. Drops in at Glebe Cottage as he passes (or in winter does paper-work in office).
8.00	Comes in for breakfast, having set men on.
8.45	Sorts out post, writes letters, telephones vet, merchants, etc.
9.30	Goes out on to farm.
11.00	Cup of coffee if near home.
1pm	Lunch.
2.00	Out again.
5.00	Calls in to see cowman and possibly lends hand; wanders round yard checking on what has been done and what needs doing tomorrow.
5.45	Goes in.
6.15	Supper.
7.00	Out for meeting, watching television, reading, etc.

The note included the following explanation: 'This is the timetable for the non-hectic times of year. During drilling, silage-making, hay-making and corn harvest this routine would tend to go by the board. Lunch and supper are flexible occasions with this type of family. Normally Phil would be likely to have his main meal at lunch-time and a glorified high tea at 6.15. However if he is out at lunch-time (market, NFU or magistrate's work, etc) or if Jill is out, or if they are entertaining, they would tend to have the main meal in the evening. Phil would have a lot of meetings to go to (he would be out two or three nights a week) and so is likely to keep the evenings free when possible.'

So in some ways the average farmer's life has changed dramatically over thirty years and in others it remains comfortingly similar, but throughout it all has been The Archers; at first advising, educating, informing, at times taking a lead, and latterly reflecting, questioning, providing a nightly forum for an exchange of ideas. Because alongside the developments in agriculture since 1951 there has been a tremendous growth in means of communication to farmers, which has relieved the programme to some extent of its original obligations. The Ministry of Agriculture's advisory team has been matched and in places overtaken by those of the commercial firms and marketing organizations. You can have your farm's data put through a computer by ICI or your dairy herd monitored by BOCM-Silcock. Fison will send a man out to tell you if your winter wheat needs spraying and Bibby's expert will call and advise on pig nutrition. No sugar beet grower looks these days to The Archers for tips on pre-emergence sprays. He picks up the telephone and gets the fieldsman from the local sugar factory to drop in. The Meat and Livestock Commission will weigh your beef cattle, the Milk Marketing Board will test your milk. And if it is financial advice you want, the banks are fighting to give it – the Midland Bank's agricultural team, for example, has grown so big these days that it takes a double-page spread of *Farmers Weekly* to fit them all in. And if you do not trust commercial interests, firms of consultants have been sprouting like mushrooms in a warm, damp autumn.

But if Ambridge is no longer the centre of agricultural education, it is certain that very little happens in farming which is not mirrored there sooner or later. Whatever goes on in the village must take place against an authentic agricultural background and, what's more, one which is changing and developing realistically season by season, year by year. When Godfrey Baseley started The Archers in 1951 he kept a model of Brookfield Farm in the Birmingham studios, with tiny cows and pigs, each representing a proportion of Dan's stock. Since I took over the agricultural editing of the series from Godfrey in the early seventies I have done the same thing – using not a toy farm but a paper one. And not just one farm but several. I do budgets for the four main holdings in Ambridge – Brookfield (Phil Archer); Home Farm (Brian Aldridge); Bridge Farm (Tony Archer); and Willow Farm (Mike Tucker) – and once a year I spend half a day with the farm management staff at the West Midlands headquarters of the Ministry of Agriculture, going through the figures, checking on cropping and stocking plans, cash flows, labour requirements and so on for four totally mythical farms. How big a beef enterprise could Brian manage without taking on another man? Should Tony go for the 100 cows or perhaps hold it at 80 and go on growing some corn? Can Phil afford to house his sheep? What ought Mike to do with his surplus acres? Would Tony have cash difficulties? Can Mike manage on the proceeds from his milk round? Will Phil put off a holiday this year? Is Brian likely to buy a mini-computer?

There's always some clever chap ready to trip you up – like the one who wrote and asked why Haydn Evans had built such a big milking parlour at Willow Farm for such a small herd. A rich man's indulgence, I replied; he wanted to do the best for his son (who repaid him by hopping off to Canada) and rather overdid it.

When I became involved with The Archers I felt the farming pattern had become too unbalanced, with Ralph Bellamy and his huge 3,500 acre farm; Dan and Phil with Brookfield – at that time 400 acres; and no central smaller farm to reflect the average which in 1972 stood at only 109 acres. Bellamy's holding was too big and there was no identifiable one small enough. I suggested two things: splitting up the Bellamy empire and carving out of it a central, more credible (for the Ambridge area) large holding of 1,500 acres which we then sold to Brian Aldridge, and creating a small farm of 100 acres which we moved Tony into and which is now occupied by Mike Tucker on a landlord/tenant partnership. Tony now rents a farm from the remains of the Bellamy estate.

These are the details in 1980 of the four main holdings in Ambridge.

BROOKFIELD – Phil Archer

465 acres, owner-occupied (including 30 acres bought in 1979 at £1,725 an acre with an Agricultural Mortgage Corporation mortgage).

Stocking:	Milking cows	110	
	Young stock	85	
	Sows	60	(1,000 pigs a year fattened to bacon)
	Ewes	300	
Cropping:		*Acres*	
	Cereals	200	
	Grass	265	
Labour:	Phil (when busy, relief milking, etc)		
	Graham Collard (cowman)		
	Jethro Larkin		
	Neil Carter (mainly pigs)		
	Fred Wakefield		
	David Archer		
	Dan (pottering)		

With David coming home from college, Phil is developing the farm and tightening up on his management which had begun to slip. His future plans, in addition to increasing the ewe flock this year from 70 to 300, include going in for potatoes. The Potato Marketing Board has granted him a quota of 11 acres for 1981 with the probability of an increase to 33 acres by 1983. He plans to join a local farmers' group to share planting and harvesting equipment and for marketing. Like many farmers, he has had to curtail his plans due to the increase in the interest rate, since, in common with most, he farms on an overdraft. He will not be increasing the milking herd, but trying to improve performance from existing cows. On ADAS (Agricultural Development and Advisory Service) advice he has given up maize as being too uncertain a crop on his land.

HOME FARM – Brian Aldridge
1,500 acres, owner-occupied with low mortgage charge.

Stocking:	Ewes	600	(200 lambing January; 400 March/April)
	Beef cattle	60	(nucleus of bigger herd)
Cropping:		*Acres*	
	Cereals	950	
	Oilseed rape	150	
	Sugar beet	100	
	Grassland	220	(100 for herbage seed)
	Woodland	80	

Labour: Brian (who takes his coat off at busy times)
Working foreman
Shepherd (plus student help at lambing)
3 tractor drivers
1 boy

Brian is in a strong position having sold a smaller farm, partly for development, in the Home Counties and bought Home Farm with the proceeds. Having failed to get into pigs in 1979 (due to local opposition to a big piggery and general frustration) he decided to go in for beef and has acquired Phil Archer's Friesian and Friesian crosses as a nucleus of what will eventually be a multiple suckler herd.

BRIDGE FARM – Tony Archer

140 acres plus 10 acres accommodation land near village.
Rented farm, rent around £30 an acre but increase due in 1981.

Stocking:	Milking cows	80	
	Young stock	50	
	Sows	6	(selling weaners)
	Hens	100	(Pat's pin-money)
Cropping:		Acres	
	Barley	25	
	Grassland	125	
Labour:	Tony		
	Malcolm		
	Percy Jordan (part-time)		
	Pat (part-time)		

Tony is worried about the EEC milk surplus and his reliance on dairying. His pig venture is a modest reflection of his concern. He cannot make up his mind whether to increase his herd to 100 so that he would be in a stronger position were farm milk quotas to be applied or whether to diversify into something else, perhaps rearing his own bull calves for beef.

WILLOW FARM – Mike Tucker

100 acres on a landlord/tenant partnership with Haydn Evans.

Stocking:	Milking cows	48	(Ayrshires)
	Young stock	30	
Cropping:		Acres	
	Barley	30	
	Kale	6	
	Grassland	64	
Labour:	Mike		
	Betty (part-time)		

Mike's agreement with his landlord can be unscrambled at six months' notice, so he has not the security of a normal tenant. On the other hand, as an ex-farm worker he has been glad of the opportunity of getting into a farm and of access to Haydn's capital. He sells some of his milk as Green Top on his milk-round, getting rid of the excess to Borchester Dairies and buying back Channel Island and pasteurized milk, cream and other dairy produce for sale on his round. He knows he is under-stocked but, being cautious, would rather sell off some hay than borrow to increase his herd.

In addition to these farms there are several other key holdings:

GRANGE FARM (Joe Grundy) 120 acres rented from the Bellamy Estate. Recently gone back into dairying.

AMBRIDGE FARM (Ken and Mary Pound) 150 acres rented from the Bellamy Estate. Herd of Jerseys, hens in batteries, farm shop.

SAWYER'S FARM, run with HEYDON FARM by Andrew Sinclair on behalf of the Bellamy Estate, with two 120-cow dairy herds.

VALLEY FARM, also taken in hand by the Bellamy Estate and used to rear young stock and grow cereals for dairy herd.

Keeping the scriptwriters in touch with what is going on in farming has become more difficult over the years partly because of the increasing complexity of agriculture and partly because of the speed of turnover of writers. When the programme started, farming was an easier business to comprehend and for the first ten or eleven years of its life it had the same two script writers. Farming in the eighties is incomparably more complex and none of those writing in the programme's twenty-ninth year was writing two years earlier.

Skilled as they undoubtedly are as writers, they cannot have the same deep knowledge of Ambridge agriculture and The Archers ethos as those involved in the earlier days. Twelve men and women have had a go at writing The Archers since I joined the team in 1972, many of whom do not know hay from a bull's foot and would not claim to. All of this makes greater demands on the agricultural editor, a fact borne out by a flip through my files of notes sent to the team over the years which have of necessity grown longer and more detailed as the influx of new writers has increased.

Many people assume that my job consists of reading the scripts and changing 'bullocks' to 'heifers' or crossing out 'ploughing' and inserting 'harrowing'. In fact, if I have done my job properly, there should be very little work to do on the scripts. I like to feed the agricultural material in at the monthly script meetings and reinforce it with notes sent to the producer and all the writers. There is a lot of give and take between producer, writers and agricultural editor.

Sometimes the action is fitted round the farming and sometimes it is the other way round. What we are trying to do all the time is bring the agriculture in as naturally as possible and wherever possible make it play a positive role in the dramatic development.

I mentioned warble fly control earlier and this provides a good illustration of the way in which the public interest can be served while at the same time enhancing the dramatic content of the serial. The Ministry of Agriculture is trying to eradicate warble flies, which do a great deal of harm to cattle production and the quality of hides. It is a subject which we would like to reflect in The Archers without getting the characters to plough through the Ministry handouts as would have happened in the early days of the programme. We therefore devised a story on the following lines:

Brian buys some beef cattle from Phil which should have been treated to prevent warble infestation the previous autumn. In the summer he notices the tell-tale bumps appearing on some of their backs, showing that the warble grubs are active beneath the skin. He has to get the cows in and dress them again – an expensive business. Phil assures him that they were all done in November but, on reflection, remembers that in his panic over buying his new land one batch probably got overlooked.

Here we have a minor but useful story which gives an opportunity to draw attention to the importance of getting rid of warbles and tells the listener something about the pest, as well as providing a nice scene or two leaving the usually infallible Phil with a red face, which he later redeems by giving Brian half a pig for his deep freeze.

My notes to the writers vary from a couple of lines to pages. One memo (I was embarrassed to see on reading through my files) simply said: 'People who ride horses call it "riding". "Horse-riding" and "horse-back riding" are terms used by people who don't do it.' On the other hand the notes for Tony's takeover of Bridge Farm and Mike's concurrent move into Willow Farm and all the knock-on effects throughout Ambridge ran to ten pages, with a great deal of detail on the physical and financial involvement of the two main parties and including a suggested timescale of events running over more than twelve months.

You may wonder why the writers are not left to do more of their own agricultural research. I think the short answer is that it is just more practicable if I do it and feed it to all the parties concerned *after* – and this is vital – *after* it has been chewed over and accepted in principle at a script conference. I would certainly never try to impose an agricultural story on the writers. What I endeavour to do is either to suggest what ought to be happening and find ways in which we

can work it into the development of the plot, or to contrive agricultural validity for something which the writers themselves want to do
with a character.

'Could Joe Grundy have a flock of sheep?' I might be asked by a
writer who desperately wanted to write a lambing sequence at
Grange Farm.

'Highly unlikely,' I would be forced to answer, in view of the fact
that we have spent a lot of time establishing Joe as a man who has
not got a sound fence on his farm.

If the writer persisted because it was important to him or her, I
would probably say: 'Okay, but they'll have to keep breaking out or
you'll have to make it clear that Eddie and Joe have spent hours
stopping all the gaps in the hedges.'

Or I might say, 'Look, it's time Neil was moving on – he has been
on the same farm since he started as an apprentice in 1973, we've
shown him to be ambitious, he ought to be looking for a job on
another farm and Phil ought to be helping him.' This would almost
certainly be greeted by howls of protest from the producer and
writers, who do not want to lose Neil, one of the most popular
characters, at any price. So we would compromise by perhaps allow-
ing Neil to get restive and having Phil reassure him about his prospects at Brookfield.

When a writer goes off at a tangent and decides to develop the
agricultural content on his own it almost always causes trouble. He
may, for example, go to a demonstration or read an article about
synchronized mating of ewes and decide that this would make a nice
story for Dan, without realizing that an old age pensioner with a
small hobby flock of ewes would be just about the most improbable
person to go in for this practice. The last thing Dan wants is all his
ewes lambing the same day. What is more, we are saddled with it for
ever more unless Dan abandons it. And if he gives it up, as I would
have to advise that he should, how do we explain it in the story
without either discrediting the value of the technique or making Dan
seem a fool for going in for it in the first place? It is very easy to
introduce things into The Archers; not so easy to get rid of them.

There are two tools which I have provided for the writers to help
them bring farming into the Ambridge scene in a practical and topical way. One is The Archers' Agricultural Calendar which shows
week by week what is going on with the whole range of crops and
livestock. All a writer has to do is to lay a ruler down the chart for
the week for which he is writing to see what is happening. He would
find, for example, if he were writing for the third week in June, that
Brian could be spraying sugar beet, Phil shearing, Tony haymaking,

Mike top-dressing, Carol spraying apples, and so on, any of which could be used to add topical agricultural colour to a scene. And backing up the calendar, the writers have notes on a long list of common farm situations ranging from changing teat-cup liners to unblocking drains, from earmarking calves to laying concrete, which, again, can be used as authentic background.

But despite all of this, we are still constantly being told that there is not enough farming in The Archers, the assumption being that there used to be a great deal more. I feel there is an element of 'those long hot summers we used to have' about the complaint. In other words I think there is as much farming as there used to be. Perhaps it is less discernible because it is woven into the fabric of the scripts so skilfully by the writers these days that it is not always so apparent, but it is also true that farming has changed in a way that makes it more difficult to write about for a non-farming audience. It is not as easy to get so interested in cow number 95 – which is identical with numbers 85 and 75 – as it was in the old days with Mabel who was an individual. And a lot of Phil's 'farming' these days is done with his bank manager, his accountant, his solicitor, the man from the AMC (Agricultural Mortgage Corporation) and various other faceless characters who would not come into our listeners' category of farming.

But the basic complaint, that there isn't as much farming in The Archers as there used to be, does not really stand up to close examination. According to Godfrey Baseley, once the series had taken off in a big way they settled down to an overall formula of ten per cent farming, twenty per cent 'birds and bees' (material about the countryside in general) and seventy per cent entertainment. I think we can claim to exceed our ten per cent most weeks.

'Where do *you* get all the information from?' I am asked from time to time. 'You can't possibly carry it all round in your head.' This is absolutely right, although I do keep closely in touch with agricultural developments through my work as a producer of 'real' farming programmes. Godfrey Baseley believed in going right to the top and had frequent meetings with the Minister of Agriculture and the President of the National Farmers' Union before deciding on Ambridge's farming policy. It is a tribute to the influence of the programme over the years that people right at the top of the farming tree were always ready to help him personally. Without in any way reflecting on the wisdom of the leaders, I have always found it more fruitful to gather my material at a lower and, usually, more local level, from the County Agricultural Adviser, the Divisional Veterinary Officer, the regional Milk Marketing Board office and so on.

Occasionally I need to go nearer the top – to find out from the British Sugar Corporation, for example, whether Brian really ought to double his acreage or to ask the Potato Marketing Board whether it would be likely to give Phil a potato quota. One feature which characterizes virtually every inquiry I make is the genuine warmth and interest and desire to help of the person at the other end of the telephone. The Archers has apparently lost none of its charisma over the years.

Stories of the programme's impact are legion. Godfrey Baseley recalls that when he decided that it was time for Dan to change to Friesians in the fifties there was uproar among Shorthorn breeders, some of whom went so far as to question whether the BBC Charter allowed a programme to threaten their livelihoods. On another occasion, a throwaway remark by the Ambridge vet to Doris to the effect that a spot of rock sulphur in her dog's water might help him withstand the heat better had a dramatic effect. 'You couldn't get a ha'porth of rock sulphur anywhere by the end of the week,' according to Godfrey. More recently, when Brian suggested lightheartedly to Phil how he could fiddle his application for a Farm and Horticultural Development Scheme Grant, the programme was scarcely off the air before I received a call from one of the Ministry of Agriculture's top officials, who was only slightly mollified by my assurance that it was made very much tongue-in-cheek.

No one will ever know what effect The Archers has had on developments in farming and the countryside, in relationships between town and country and between producers and consumers. We shall never know the extent, but I think we can safely say that it has been a beneficial one.

The Eighties

CHAPTER 10

The Future

by William Smethurst

Once upon a time there was a jolly farmer and his jolly apple-cheeked wife, and they had two strong horses called Blossom and Boxer, and their younger son played tennis a lot and loved a girl called Grace . . .

Thirty years and 7,800 episodes later, and the story continues to unravel, night after night. Not the greatest story ever told, perhaps, but certainly the longest. In his *Defence of Poesy*, Sir Philip Sidney wrote of 'A tale which holdeth children from play, and old men from the chimney corner,' and that is what The Archers has striven to be down the years, not without some modest success. One of the most frequent letters to arrive on the producer's desk is the one that starts: 'Why can't The Archers be like it used to be . . .' But what exactly do these listeners want? The return of Mike Daly MC, perhaps, who was last heard of in 1954 when a certain Baroness Czorva carried him off on a secret service mission? Or a return to the violence of the past – because Ambridge has certainly been a terribly violent place, with Tom Forrest killing poachers, Doris and Jack Woolley being left unconscious by robbers, jet planes crashing (twice), kidnapping, arson, sabotage and innumerable car crashes. The personal accident rate, too, has been incredibly high. Dan's shoulder, alone, has been damaged by a farm implement, dropped on from a great height by a cow, and crushed by a beam in the church belfry. Hundreds of Ambridge residents must have been rushed into Borchester General Hospital over the years, two have been consigned to the county

June Spencer (Peggy Archer) and Chris Gittins (Walter Gabriel) wait to
record in Studio 3 at Pebble Mill.

hospital for nervous and mental disorders, and members of the
Archer family have been curiously prone to 'acting strangely', and
wandering round the countryside by themselves (Doris, Phil and Jill
in one year alone).

The moral tone of the programme has certainly changed, but for
better or worse? In 1951 Christine was having an affair with her
married boss at Borchester Dairies, in 1967 Jennifer had an illegitimate baby by an Irishman, and in the early seventies Nora McAuley
moved in with and became pregnant by an alcoholic gamekeeper
who had a wife and two children elsewhere. In 1980, it is true, Eva
the au pair girl slept with PC Coverdale – but it was only a few weeks
before their wedding, and was a gentler, more humorous story than
the sordid passions of yesteryear.

The fact is that those listeners who look back to some idyllic,
peaceful Ambridge where nobody every quarrelled or did anything
nasty are looking back to a programme that never existed. The original formula was to take the most extravagant stories – violence,
intrigue, human strife and passion – and juxtapose them with cosy
scenes in the kitchen at Brookfield Farm. It worked brilliantly
through the fifties and most of the sixties, and only went wrong

when the cosy scenes became cloying and the extravagant stories became outrageous. Nelson Gabriel's strange involvement in the Borchester mail van robbery, the absurd and impossible kidnapping of Adam Travers-Macy . . . an everyday story of countryfolk? Well it never was *that* exactly, but the sixties were cruel years for The Archers, and the programme was floundering helplessly by the time it entered its third decade.

It was shaken and mauled, but it survived, and somewhere along the line it became an institution; part of the British way of life. The stories sobered down (the 1975 attempt on the postbus by bandits with iron bars was the last flicker of the fifties) and people stopped hunting foxes, or drinking more than a half of bitter when they went to the pub. Eventually it acquired a fashionable image. Ambridge Supporters Clubs sprang up, and 'Doris For Queen Mum' teashirts appeared at universities. It became – and remains – a cult among male journalists who fantasize about Shula, and among a public with a new affection for nostalgia and compost-grown vegetables.

Where does it go next?

Angela Piper (Jennifer Aldridge) and Charles Collingwood (Brian Aldridge) recording in the studio.

Writers today are given a simple brief: to tell a story (holding children from play, and old men from the chimney corner) which reflects life in an English village and the values of people who live there. This has always been a basic element of the programme. The Archers has always been – though not always prepared to admit – the voice of the Shires, conservative, sensible and not particularly egalitarian. It has always radiated the belief that there is nowhere really in the world but England, and nowhere in England but a particular corner of Worcestershire and Warwickshire. (It could just as easily, of course, be Dorset or Shropshire.)

Over the years The Archers has matured, like a good cheese, and the gutsy *Dick Barton* stories of the old Light Programme days have been largely replaced by a more subtle social comedy more appropriate to Radio Four. (Not entirely, though. Already in 1980 Tony has been struck down with tetanus and injected with a South American 'curare' drug, and Mark has been kicked by a dying deer and collapsed at Grey Gables.) The days when The Archers was afraid to mention politics in any context, called Land Rovers 'field reconnaissance vehicles', and banished the South Borsetshire Hunt to North Borset to pacify the anti-hunting lobby are over. The programme today has been described as, 'middle-class soap-opera with the philosophy of the *Daily Telegraph* and a sinister appeal to readers of the *Guardian*.' It is certainly true that the *Guardian* publishes more letters about the programme than any other newspaper!

The biggest change in the last few years has been in the way the programme is written. When it started, Geoffrey Webb and Ted Mason wrote all the scripts, and continued to do so for years. New writers came in, and once in, stayed, their contracts renewed if they wished as a matter of course. Now, however, writers are invited to join the team for six months, the assumption being that they will then wish to do other work, and perhaps return later.

This policy has had two marked effects: enormous problems over continuity, and a constant demand for new writers. Whether or not it has dramatically improved the quality of scripts – the purpose of the change – only the listeners can judge.

But radio is a writer's medium. Producers, editors and controllers write memos – writers write scripts. It was Geoffrey Webb and Ted Mason who created the programme, and it is the present writing team – four of them at any given time – that make The Archers live and breathe today.

What makes a good Archers writer? Well, ideally he should live in Worcestershire or South Warwickshire (if only so that he can get to script meetings easily, and dash re-writes to the studio quickly in

In the studio, 1980. Production secretary Diane Culverhouse, director Clare Taylor, studio manager Marc Decker and grams operator Julia Bache.

emergencies) and should be able to write with humour and understanding about the countryside and people around him. He should be able to reflect rural society, from a pub darts match to a hunt ball, with perception and sympathy. If he's an officer in the Yeomanry, rides to hounds, and runs the tombola every year at the Conservative Garden Fête, then so much the better.

All this crumbles to dust when you realize that the present writing team includes Helen Leadbeater, who works part-time as a solicitor's clerk in Notting Hill; Mary Cutler who lives in central Birmingham; Alan Bower whose home is in deepest Kent; and James Robson who resides in North Yorkshire. Only Tim Rose-Price, who lives in a cottage in the Cotswolds, conforms to the ideal – and even he has no noticeable interest in the Yeomanry, hunt or tombola stall.

In the end it is the quality of writing that counts, and the present team were taken on because they are among the best people writing for radio today. What is encouraging is that they *want* to write for The Archers. Novelist Susan Hill is more used to hearing her plays broadcast on Radio Three, and James Robson's stage-play *Factory Birds* was performed by the Royal Shakespeare Company and won him the *Evening Standard*'s 'Most Promising Playwright' award. Helen Leadbeater and Mary Cutler, the terrible twins of the writing team, are young and clever (they were both on University Challenge, but fortunately were not asked questions about farming). Tim Rose-Price has recently been working on a libretto for a promenade concert. These writers all find something peculiarly satisfying in being able to shape events in Ambridge for a week, then return a month later to shape them a bit more. Television soap operas have 'storyline writers' and carefully laid-down plots, but an Archers writer has the freedom to do anything – anything, that is, except kill characters off.

That sort of decision is reserved for meetings in the Pink Sitting Room (hire charge £7·50), which is in a pleasant Cotswold hotel, has chintzy chairs, a roaring fire in the late autumn, and french windows that open on to a garden full of stocks, delphiniums and lupins in the early summer. Every six months or so the writers meet there, and

Sara Coward (Caroline Bone) and Richard Darrington (Mark Hebden)
sharing a joke.

over afternoon tea and cream cakes, gentle voices can be heard murmuring . . .

'Ralph Bellamy's always moaning about having a heart attack, let's give him one . . .'

'Perhaps we could kill Lizzie Larkin off in a car crash . . .'

Or, only slightly less terrible: 'Let's send them to Guernsey for a holiday.' (The Archers is such an English programme – though token Celts are brought in from time to time to fill minor roles – that Guernsey is regarded as the equivalent of Siberia. Even Dan and Doris were once held captive there for two months when Doris developed bronchitis.)

But writers are not naturally vicious or bloodthirsty. There is a marked reluctance to get rid of anybody. Every character has a following among the public, and deaths are a messy business and generally bad for trade. Younger listeners might accept the demise of a central character with equanimity, but older listeners are not cheered. No, characters are only moved or killed out of necessity. Some have to go to make room for new characters (the budget only allows for the casting of a limited number of people each week) and others go because the actor or actress wants to leave, and re-casting is not considered practicable.

A certain realism must also be maintained. Many of the main, central characters who were middle-aged when the programme started are now in their eighties, and have slowly been moved to the background. For three years at least the key stories have been about younger characters (young, admittedly, meaning under sixty-five) and the listeners themselves are younger than they were.

The stories themselves emerge in a haphazard fashion. What shall we do about Clarrie and Eddie? Ought Brian to have put his beef cattle on a multi-suckling system? If Dan tries to do too much with the sheep on Lakey Hill will he have a heart attack? What actually *did* happen between Caroline Bone and Terry Barford? (An hour's discussion follows here, on whether or not a twenty-six-year-old sprig of the aristocracy would really fancy a nineteen-year-old squaddie.) Appeals for publicity from numerous causes are considered and generally, if regretfully, turned down. Jill is already doing Meals on Wheels and Peggy is local secretary for the Church of England Children's Society. Pressure groups for equal opportunities, race relations and homosexual equality are rejected more firmly. We are writing about a typical English village, after all, not reflecting what might be considered to be fashionable metropolitan causes.

Crises arise inevitably over continuity. The Archers' filing system will tell you instantly that Doris did not like egg custard in 1957, but

Shula (Judy Bennett) and David (Nigel Carrivick).

it is fallible in other areas. Why, for example, have we brought David home for good, when two years ago we sent him on a three-year course at agricultural college? (He obviously changed his mind about the course he wanted to do.)

But nobody really controls the direction of the programme, at least not in any cool, analytical way. The producer certainly does not, and the writers could never be mistaken for Olympian Gods, as they sit over their coffee cups with glazed expressions, and fail utterly to respond to the question: 'Surely somebody can think of a story for Sid and Polly?'

In the end they go away to their typewriters, back to their endless game of consequences, armed with a storyline they can safely ignore, and probably nurturing some secret story that will involve one of their favourite characters bashing one of their least favourite characters.

The story seems to have a will of its own, but perhaps something can be said of the future with tolerable confidence. The programme is now centred firmly on its four main farms: Brookfield, with Phil, Jill, Shula and David; Home Farm with Jennifer and Brian; Bridge Farm with Pat and Tony, and Grange Farm with the awful Grundys. It contains more farming material than ever before (even if listeners refuse to believe it); and it remains a programme with a basically

The Brookfield family in 1980: Patricia Green (Jill), Nigel Carrivick (David), Norman Painting (Phil) and Judy Bennett (Shula).

optimistic view of life. It has also become more of a social comedy, and if the current team – writers, directors and actors – are trying to present a slightly more significant commentary on rural life than in the past, they are doing it quietly and modestly.

A generation has passed in Ambridge. Phil and Jill are the same age as Dan and Doris were in 1951. Shula and David are like Christine and Phil were then. Joe Grundy bears a marked resemblance to the Walter Gabriel of early years – an inefficient, occasionally drunken farmer with a tearaway son. There's an attractive, rather posh girl in the village – not Carol Grey, but Caroline Bone.

The road lies open! It only needs a young college lecturer to come round the corner in a green caravan, and it can all start again . . .

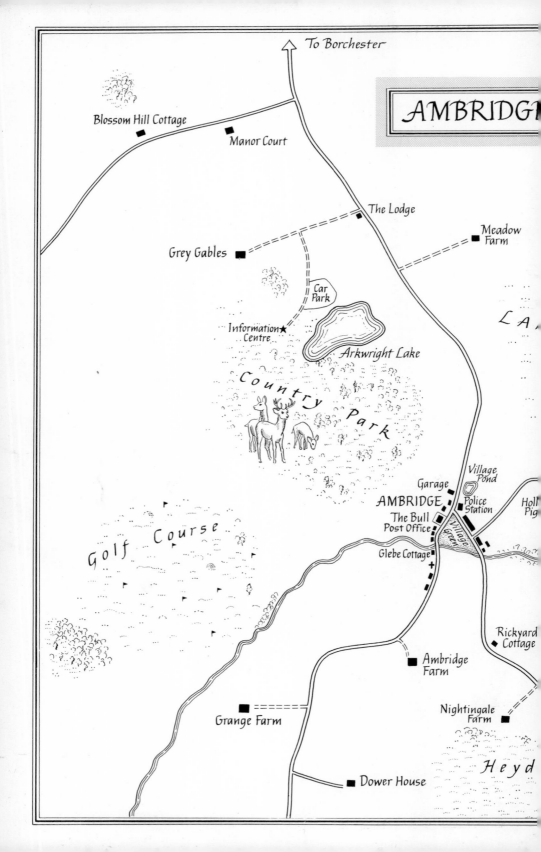